The 15 Minute Master

How to Make Everything Better
15 Minutes at a Time

Mary Fran Bontempo

Little Beach Press

For Dave, David, Laura, Megan, Kelly, Mike, Jimmy, Emma, Luca, Jackson, Kaia, Nathan and baby Malatesta

My reasons for everything.

Praise for
The 15 Minute Master and
Mary Fran Bontempo

"Mary Fran made me laugh, again. That was no surprise. But what I wasn't expecting was the tangible process she gave me to just do life better. And all with a compelling and emotional story. A must-read."

Jennifer L Croneberger

Author of *These Five Words Are Mine*, Award-Winning 3-time TEDx Speaker, Compassionate Leadership Specialist, www.thefivewords.com

"With humor and grace, Mary Fran brings a framework for us to walk THROUGH the storm, not around it. We've all had or maybe are having moments in our lives when we want to close our eyes, cover our ears, and wake up on the other side when the sun is shining, and life is good. But if we do so, where does the learning go? When do we grow, expand, become more than we've ever been before? Mary Fran's 15-minute strategy is like a holistic pain killer to be able to bear the pain we sometimes feel but that we know will help us grow into our best version. This is a MUST read!"

Dolores Hirschmann

Speaker, Coach, Strategist, Founder: Masters in Clarity, www.mastersinclarity.com

"Mary Fran uses her own personal experiences to provide others with a simple, effective method for managing both crises and everyday dilemmas. Although grounded in heavy subject matter, I found the book to be humor-filled, forthright and honest. The three-question formula is easy to understand and can help make life better one action step at a time!"

Fran Hauser
Media executive, startup investor, best-selling author of *The Myth of the Nice Girl: Achieving a Career You Love Without Becoming a Person You Hate,* www.franhauser.com

"From the moment I met Mary Fran Bontempo, I noticed three attributes: integrity, transparency and humor. Her ability to bring all three to every conversation was something I immediately respected in her. Her latest book, *The 15 Minute Master—How to Make Everything Better 15 Minutes at a Time,* incorporates all three. The ability to bring honesty, clarity and levity to times of tragedy are a gift to any of us going through tough times. A great read!"

Susan Rocco
Women to Watch Media, Founder and Host, www.women2watch.net

"The 15 Minute Master is masterful. Mary Fran hits the nail on the head with this sharp, to the point and in-your-face approach to tackling real life problems, and she does it with a warm and funny undertone. The beauty of her message is this...while written from the view of an addict's mother, the 15-minute approach speaks to us all. Her steps to making any situation 'better, not perfect' are real, relatable and doable. 15 minutes. A better life is just minutes away!"

Beth Allen
Founder of HIP Chicks. Speaker, DIY Expert, Media Contributor, https://diyhipchicks.com

"As the saying goes, 'This, too, shall pass.' Mary Fran's book, The 15 Minute Master, will help you get through the challenge till it passes. Based on her personal experience dealing with an overwhelming situation, Mary Fran provides simple and impactful advice on how to catch your breath and chisel away at life's occasional crises. This easy read comes packed with practical advice, and, of course, the humor you'd expect from our favorite 'not ready for granny panties' author. Another must-read gem!"

Theresa Hummel-Krallinger
Trainer/ Management Consultant, Motivational Speaker, Humorist, Founder, High Five Performance, https://www.highfiveperformance.com

"Once again Mary Fran has written a smart book with great warmth which comes from her heart and her own experiences. She generously shares how she survived an extremely stressful and overwhelming time in her life by creating a simple but highly effective method which paves the way for any of us to survive a difficult period in our lives or to make our everyday lives more focused and purposeful. Mary Fran's legendary humor is sprinkled throughout the book, which creates an even more enjoyable reading experience. When my patients are going through a tough time, I tell them to take action...Mary Fran shows us how!"

Dr. Ellen Faulkner
Founder/Owner—The Bucks County Psychotherapy Group, Leadership Coach & Consultant with The Global Consulting Partnership, www.buckstherapygroup.com

"This book really resonated with me. We have all been through challenges and it is so important to help others not only by sharing our story but with concrete compensation strategies. Mary Fran addresses an important issue that many are unwilling to talk about. We need more of this."

Jennifer Lynn Robinson,
Esquire CEO Purposeful Networking, President: FemCity Philadelphia, www.purposefulnetworking.com

"Life happens and sometimes it happens big time. I saw the title and thought 15 minutes? Really? But then I read it and I felt relieved, validated, and motivated to move forward despite the big life situation. I can do 15 minutes. I can get a sense of accomplishment in 15 minutes even if it's only baby steps and feel less overwhelmed, less guilty, and more empowered. This is not a self-help book that's overwhelming to even start. It's not a system that you'll set up and quit using. I can keep on doing 15 minutes."

Denice Whiteley
Product Launch Concierge, www.DeniceWhiteley.com

"Mary Fran Bontempo, through her own horrific life experience, has created a tool for all of us to use to not only face the obstacles we experience on our life journey, but to manage and overcome them with grace, perseverance and humor. No matter how big or how small, or how many people are involved in the web of turmoil you experience, Mary Fran's 15 Minute Master program will enlighten you and give you the strength to carry on, having the tools you need to survive any situation with love, dignity, and eventually, joy. Brilliant."

Robyn Graham
Branding Expert, Photographer, www.robyngrahamphotography.com

"Well, she's done it again! MaryFran Bontempo's third book, The 15 Minute Master, does not disappoint. She reflects on a life-changing crisis, douses it with humor, and shares how she and her family survived (and thrived!)15 minutes at a time. Whether at a personal or professional crossroads, or even just beginning a new project, the 15 Minute Master system shows you how breaking the process into just 15 minutes can be a game changer. It really was for me!"

Kathy Marcino
Business Communications Coach,
specializing in Workplace Conflict Resolution, www.KMMDISC.com

"All of us have been thrown in a pit in our lives. Many of us have a friend that will sit with us in that pit. This book is like that friend, but also there with a ladder, toolbox and roadmap to get out! 'The 15 Minute Master' feels like a continuation of Mel Robbins' 'The 5 Second Rule.' Mary Fran gives the 'brick by brick' plan to take action after taking a breath when life hits us hard, and her wit and style and 'I've been there' point of view makes readers feel like she is with us on our journey... cheering, pushing, and celebrating when we reach the other side. Read this book!"

Kristin Smedley
Speaker, Author of *Thriving Blind*, www.kristinsmedley.com

"As a communication expert, I routinely talk about how in today's environment we are so easily overwhelmed by the volume of information that comes at us each day and how as listeners we have fundamentally changed. We teach that when we as communicators make messages more bite sized, focused, and intentional they are gifts that we give our listeners. It turns out that those same elements can be gifts to ourselves. The 15 Minute Master method provides focus, helps us manage a seemingly overwhelming problem, and helps us move forward with intentional progress. These tools are essential for life in today's fast-paced world. The book outlines a simple strategy that every person should have at the ready to help navigate the unforeseen waters that the future will bring."

Dr. Patricia Scott
Communications Expert & Best-Selling Author of *Getting a Squirrel to Focus*, President & CEO of Uhmms, www.uhmms.com

"The 15 Minute Master, as a practice, enables you to take your power back in any situation by controlling your reaction to the good, the bad, the awkward, and the ugly. I have personally used this brilliance of Mary Fran Bontempo in situations of devastating crisis, profound sadness, extreme stress, and even euphoric moments. By managing your reaction with grace, you prevent further escalation of a crisis. When practiced, you turn your panic and anxiety into a determination. Once through the 15 minutes, you can applaud the accomplishment of survival and move forward with a bit of confidence, even if you are rolling into another extreme 15 minutes. I have also used the technique to enjoy the priceless moments in life that are often missed due to distraction. A must read and must practice technique for anyone wanting to take back their power and enjoy more of life's moments."

Dr. Jennifer Gardella
Social Media Expert, www.jennifergardella.com

"As a Licensed Marriage and Family Therapist, I have had the privilege of working with many clients over the years who have struggled in one way or another with addiction. What I know for sure is that addiction always has a profound effect on families. In her book, 'The 15 Minute Master—How to Make Everything Better 15 Minutes at a Time', Mary Fran Bontempo eloquently addresses her family's journey through her son's powerful heroin addiction. She speaks about the lessons they have learned along the way and does it with grace and a dose of humor. The method she developed to cope and even create a sense of peace can be used by anyone going through such a harrowing time. I will most definitely encourage my clients to read this book."

Marie R. Herbert
LMFT, Author: Get in the Muck: Reflections on Intimate Connections

"If life has just deposited you atop a snowy mountain, Mary Fran Bontempo has a pair of skis for you. During an unfolding crisis, the route to safety is scary—and the destination relative—but her step-by-step guide to sanity is a reassuring companion on the way. The only thing that would have been better, of course, is if you'd taken skiing lessons from Mary Fran ahead of time. So, even if you are one of those rare souls experiencing blissful, sunny days, please read this marvelous book NOW, while you still have time to learn how to slalom life's most heart-wrenching challenges."

Christine Marie Eberle
Author: Finding God in Ordinary Time www.christine-marie-eberle.com

Contents

Introduction

This book is not only the one everyone should read, but also the one I should have written years ago. The method outlined in The 15 Minute Master helped me get through the worst crisis in my life and enabled me to not only survive but thrive. It also helped me make everyday decisions when I was stuck, tired, or just confused about what to do and where to go. The 15 Minute Master system evolved organically, as a matter of survival. It started as my life raft and has become my go-to blueprint for creating the life I want, every day. It's how I make things better, 15 minutes at a time. It worked for me. It will work for you, too.

As the "Not Ready for Granny Panties" and the "Dirty Words" lady, I approach my work and life with humor. I write with humor because I love making people laugh, but also because, if you want to teach someone something, do it with humor. They'll remember.

Since Mother's Day 2010, everything I write is intended to teach someone something, or at least to pass on some of the lessons I've learned in a life that was sometimes not very funny at all. That Mother's Day was when I learned I was the mother of a heroin addict. My son had overdosed on a painkiller he ingested trying to get the high he got from heroin. At the hospital, the doctors told us that if they couldn't reverse the effects of the medicine, David would need a liver transplant, if he lived.

That moment changed everything about who I thought I was, what I thought I had, and where I thought I was going. One minute you're one person, the next, you're someone you don't even recognize.

The twelve hours after we got David to the hospital were crucial. You may not think it's possible to hold your breath for twelve hours; it is. When the doctor told us that David's liver test came back clear, I finally exhaled with relief, but briefly, because I knew that although my son had survived, he was still a drug addict. And I was his mother.

Nothing prepares you for the world of addiction. It's the tenth circle of Hell, and it changed everything. Every single moment of every single day for years. And none of it was fun.

Strangely, though, my husband and I did manage to laugh. Most of the time, it was a cross between a chuckle and hysteria, but still. Those moments, brief as they were, taught me to look for the light, even in the form of dark humor, which is sometimes the funniest of all, because it's born of, "Holy Hell, can you believe this sh*t? Hahahahahaha!"

In those spaces, between the panic and madness, I recognized the need for and power of humor. When we got David into treatment and I began to ever so timidly look toward the future, it became the reason my work turned toward funny.

I started the blog, "Not Ready for Granny Panties," eventually following it with a book of the same name, and then, *The Woman's Book of Dirty Words*. I've built a humor-filled brand based on practical wit and wisdom, almost all of which developed over the years of David's active addiction.

But it's this book, *The 15 Minute Master*, that reflects how I got to this point. How my husband and I got through that dark time. This book shows how I crawled through the muck and ended up on the other side, somewhat disheveled, occasionally confused (okay, frequently confused), but still standing, and frankly, not looking half-bad either.

When I wrote the first two books, I needed to laugh. I still do, and you'll laugh as you read *The 15 Minute Master*, too. But I decided it was time to backtrack a bit and share some of the pain, yes, but also the method that evolved organically, becoming the lifeline that got me through the ugliness, and that guides me through the everyday even now.

The 15 Minute Master's essential principles, message, and program were formulated by and within a crisis. Yet this book is not only for people in crisis. It's for anyone facing a challenge, a decision, or a problem with no clear, obvious solution. In sharing the method of *The 15 Minute Master*, I want to teach you that "better" is possible, in the worst of times, or when you simply don't know what to do about something. You can get through, you will survive, and I think I can help, which is the only way any of what we went through with David means something—if we can help other people.

To that end, I want you to know that David is doing well. He is now what is referred to as "in recovery," which he will always be, as a former addict. At this writing, he has been clean and sober for eight years. He is the married father of three, and works in the recovery field, helping others find hope.

I thank God for him and my family every day. And while I will never say, "That experience was a blessing," because really, it sucked, it has changed my life and I want it to use it. This is the way I know how.

So welcome to *The 15 Minute Master*. I hope you like it, I hope you laugh, and I hope you learn—how to make everything better 15 minutes at a time.

Chapter 1
Why 15 Minutes?

Fifteen minutes. It was all my husband and I could manage at the height of our son's heroin addiction. "Take it one day at a time" is the usual mantra in a crisis. But there is no "usual" with addiction. No normal, no predictable, no respite to think. In the world of addiction, one day may as well be 100 years.

An addict doesn't think in terms of days. An addict thinks in terms of his next fix. Everyone around him who has become collateral damage is shackled to a version of that madness. So "one day at a time" was a fantasy. So was half a day, or even an hour. But fifteen minutes we could do. Fifteen minutes became our beacon.

When David was home, his behavior always unpredictable, we moved forward in 15-minute increments. If we got through 15 minutes without a blow-up or a crisis, we moved on to the next fifteen. If we were away from him, we took each 15-minute period as a blessed opportunity to feel "normal," going for a walk, out to lunch, or even grocery shopping, always with the phone ready in wait for the next emergency.

And when he was raging and out of control, which often happened when my husband wasn't home, I would lock myself in my bedroom for 15 minutes, waiting on the other side of the door for David to leave the house or for his anger to subside. Those 15 minutes bought me safety and a tiny measure of peace.

In the height of such a crisis, survival is crucial. It's often the only thing you can think of, and even that is more an instinctive reaction than a thought-out process. You take life in 15-minute intervals because it takes that long for you to quickly grasp what's going on and do one thing to get you through to the next 15 minutes.

One thing. The 15-minute mantra came down to that. What one thing could we do to get through to the next 15 minutes, to hang onto some sanity and keep our son alive for another day, until possibly, we could get help?

So, I became a 15 Minute Master. At first, my 15-minute mastery came from sheer desperation. I wish I could say it was a well-thought out plan, but in truth, it was simply instinct at its most basic. There's not enough time in such crisis to plan anything. Most often, you're simply reacting to the latest terror.

But by getting through the next 15 minutes, by using that time to move forward, even if forward meant just getting to the next 15 minutes, we survived. Approaching things in 15-minute bites allowed us to breathe, make decisions, take small actions to address problems, and most important, to occasionally feel normal when our world was spinning out of control.

In fact, it worked so well that it became our mantra. No matter what greeted or attacked us during a single day, we made it through by following our 15-minute formula.

Fifteen minutes is enough time to START. When hit with a crisis, the experience is so overwhelming that we don't know how to make a dent in the issue, let alone solve it. Deciding where to begin, and actually beginning, can seem impossible. Paralyzed by the experience, most of us frequently stay in a place of suffering, not believing that anything we do can make the situation better. Instead of trying, we live in that space until some outside force changes the situation. It makes us victims, hijacks our control, and leaves us frightened, miserable, and powerless.

But it doesn't have to be that way.

Fifteen minutes lets you begin to break down the mountain into a molehill. It's the first shovel of snow after a miserable February storm that will keep you stuck for days if you don't clear the driveway. It's the first bite in finishing the meal in front of you that was made by a really terrible cook whom you happen to love and would never hurt by saying, "Oh my god, this is awful!" Moving out of inertia and into action is doable in 15 minutes. You tackle it One. Single. Bite. At. A. Time.

Moving out of inertia and into action is doable in 15 minutes. You tackle it One. Single. Bite. At. Time.

I used my 15-minute periods to do whatever was necessary at the moment. Sometimes I began to plan a course of action. Sometimes I did one thing on a previously determined plan. Sometimes I immersed myself in 15 minutes of wedding gowns and fantasy by watching an episode of *Say Yes to the Dress*. (I love that show; it's gotten me through some terrible times.) Sometimes I just closed my eyes while sitting in silence on the couch; blessed silence is always in short supply when living with an out-of-control addict.

I worked my 15-minute plan knowingly and unknowingly, realizing at the end of every day that it got me through, whether I was fully aware of it or not. It provided boundaries, measures of time where I could manage, or begin to manage, the madness in my life. Soon enough, I made it my constant companion, relying on it to center me in the middle of my personal storm.

Eventually, my 15-minute plan became so much a part of me that I trotted it out for others to see. During the worst of my son's addiction, when I was simply trying to keep from drowning in chaos and pain, people would ask how I was doing. Not one to share the nasty details, I usually responded, "I'm taking life 15 minutes at a time." They responded with sympathy, but there was something else. I could almost see the "light bulb" over their heads switch on as they contemplated managing life in small bites. They would often smile ruefully and say, "Huh. Maybe I should try that."

I noticed that my 15-minute mantra, the one that was saving my sanity and my life, resonated with other people. There was something in the simplicity that transferred to my family and friends when I shared my strategy for getting through the worst time in my life. I discovered that being a 15 Minute Master could be applied beyond my own circumstances and used to help others.

When talking with friends or family about my own crises, I regularly shared what I thought of as my lifeline. I told them how my 15-minute mantra was getting me through, allowing me to formulate small actionable steps that kept me from living in a constant state of terror while waiting for the next lie, the next emergency, the next battle in what felt like an all-consuming war on our way of life.

Often, people would share their own experiences and problems, and muse that maybe my 15-minute formula could help them, too. We talked about what they could do, or sometimes not do, in the next 15 minutes to make a difference in whatever they were struggling with. The results were always the same: No matter what the issue, after applying what I would later call the basic principles of the 15 Minute Master, people not only felt better, they felt more in control.

Which brings me to what The 15 Minute Master is not—a time management formula. Too many books, theories, processes out there try to tell us how to manage our time. In crisis, time is a nebulous thing, like fog in a Stephen King novel. You can get lost. There's either too little, when things are happening so fast you can't catch your breath, or too much, like when your son is on a drug-induced rant and pounding on your locked bedroom door screaming at you, while every second feels endless.

My day rarely goes according to plan. My life simply isn't that structured. So, time management principles, though they can be helpful, don't work for me. I never strictly enforce them. I can't, and I really don't want to, which is probably the real reason they don't work. Through The 15 Minute Master, however, I get a grip on situations, I formulate plans, and I initiate action, but not on any rigorous schedule. That works for me, but if you're a time management junkie (sorry, poor choice of words), you can still use The 15 Minute Master in tandem with your schedule. In fact, the principles will clarify where to expend your energy and focus your efforts to make your time management even more efficient. (I think I need to lie down now....)

Living life at least partially within the guidelines of a 15-minute time frame actually helps to create more time, in longer stretches, for productivity, joy and the other good stuff we want life to be about. By confining our reactions to a crisis to getting through a 15-minute period, we stem the flood of what-ifs, deal with the now, and sometimes find it's not as bad as we thought. Or it is, but we can advance with the knowledge that we survived the last fifteen minutes; we'll get through the next fifteen.

I found myself thinking of 15 minutes as a "magical" time frame. So much potential lived within that contained period. Fifteen minutes could be a life raft to get through a current crisis, or a brief stretch of joy or rest inserted into a fraught day.

Fifteen minutes could *change* things.

I found myself thinking of fifteen minutes as a "magical" time frame.
Fifteen minutes could change things.

It was later, when life returned to "normal" (what exactly is that, anyway?) that I realized my 15-minute mantra had the potential to work beyond the immediacy of the moment, where it had originated. By taking the same time frame, but using it to *plan* a course of action, instead of simply reacting to a current crisis, I found myself more in control, less stressed, more proactive, and less involved in things that didn't concern me, leaving me more energy to deal with things I needed or wanted to. That was when The 15 Minute Master became a conscious system, one I had started working unconsciously, which held great potential for longer term planning and results.

When you take on The 15 Minute Master as a system while your own life is "normal," you train your mind to think and process information based on the three questions. You begin to automatically set up boundaries around situations, ask if problems are "real," and focus intently, leading to an action step and moving you forward, even if forward means rest or retreat.

Should you find yourself in crisis again (and we all will at some point), The 15 Minute Master process will kick in, and you'll find yourself quickly assessing the situation, asking yourself the three questions, and acting, in conjunction with the thought *I just have to get through the next 15 minutes.* The combined approach has been nothing short of miraculous, at least for me.

But even when you've absorbed the process of The 15 Minute Master, remember—in fact, burn into your brain—the concept of dealing with only the next 15 minutes. When you're caught in a crisis, or even challenged by daily life, recall that the present is all we really have anyway. How can you deal with, or make this moment better? No matter what the situation, 15 minutes, you can do.

So, The 15 Minute Master is actually a combination of elements. A pairing of a philosophy encouraging us to take life 15 minutes at a time, particularly when in crisis, and a system which, when worked consistently, allows us to plan, problem solve, and make that life better, one 15-minutes process at a time.

For me, The 15 Minute Master began as an *Oh my god, my life is out of control and I've got to do something* formula. That's often where it starts. Loss of control doesn't sit well with me, or with most of us. If we're honest, we'll admit that much of life is out of our control, which is totally unsettling, particularly when it seems like people in charge of the big stuff are crazier than we are. That's when it is even more necessary for us to feel as if we can control our immediate world, or at least part of it.

**When you're caught in a crisis,
or even challenged by daily life,
recall that the present is all we really have anyway.**

**How can you deal with,
or make this moment better?**

**No matter what the situation,
15 minutes, you can do.**

The 15 Minute Master gives you back some control. Sometimes, even better, it lets you know when you're running into a brick wall and you should really stop, or at least put on a helmet, because it's going to keep hurting if you don't. It's monumentally useful for folks in crisis, when control is missing but desperately desired. Yet the beauty of the process is that when you incorporate it into your thoughts and actions, it transcends crisis, making everyday decisions and challenges more manageable, less stressful, and less emotionally fraught.

While we're at it, let's ditch the idea that The 15 Minute Master is a program, or a prolonged process, or something new you have to study in order to gain proficiency. I don't know about you, but I'm tired of climbing giant learning curves. There's a ton of stuff out there that I COULD learn about; I just don't want to. There are other things that interest me, and while I'm all about making life easier and better, I don't want to invest my precious money, energy, or time into learning the latest "thing" that I'm going to do for a few weeks and then drop like I did the Keto diet. (Seriously, who can live without carbs?)

I promise you, The 15 Minute Master is EASY. While I may have to use the words "process" and "program" for lack of better terms, you will not be subjected to learning complex systems, rules, or structures. I don't have time for that; neither do you. Even if I did, the 15 Minute Master is about breaking things down into manageable bites, keeping things simple, and passing off emotional burdens when at all possible. The 15 Minute Master is designed to give you more time, not deprive you of it.

As you become a 15 Minute Master, you'll not only get better at handling life's challenges, you'll learn how to set boundaries. When in crisis, the what-ifs and what-should-I-dos can crowd our heads like tired commuters vying for a spot on the train at the end of a long day. Everyone wants their space, but there's just not enough room. The same holds true with any important decision or change. What gets space in our heads and where exactly do we start?

We start by setting boundaries. By using the principles of The 15 Minute Master, you'll focus on ONE situation, ONE course of action, ONE potential outcome at a time.

The 15 Minute Master returns a measure of structure to thoughts in a brain that can resemble a pinball game, the ball bouncing off one obstacle after another, magnifying the chaos, right before the entire thing goes tilt. (I actually love playing pinball. Just not inside my head.)

The short chunk of time 15 minutes allows helps to contain the problem. By confining yourself to that one crisis, problem, or idea, you build a temporary wall around the situation, allowing you to focus, plan, and move forward. Of course, the noise will return—it's a hazard of modern life—but keeping it out 15 minutes at a time will prove life-changing.

Speaking of life-changing, let's be clear. The 15 Minute Master is not only for those in crisis. That's certainly where it started for me, but it became such a valuable tool, and so simple to use that it transferred well and quickly to other areas of life. It will for you, too, no matter who you are or what your challenges may be.

Fifteen minutes. Magical, any way you look at it.

Chapter 2
What Does "Better" Mean?

Many non-fiction books have tag lines, intended to help you know what the book is about when the title doesn't give you enough information. Kind of like *The 15 Minute Master*. The tagline for this book is, *How to Make Everything Better 15 Minutes at a Time*. But what exactly does "better" mean?

Let's start with what it doesn't mean. It doesn't mean fixed. Or solved. Or perfect. This book, in fact, no book, will give you the answers to solve all of your problems. We humans aren't privy to that information. We're destined to have to figure things out, sometimes awkwardly, sometimes slowly, and rarely perfectly. Yet, there are ways to make the process easier, and that IS what The 15 Minute Master does.

According to Merriam-Webster, "better" means improved, more attractive, favorable or commendable. Better is not as bad as it was before. Better means on the way to okay, or even to great, if you're lucky.

Better is not always instantaneous, although it can be. Sometimes you make a situation better immediately, sometimes the benefits are long-term and play out over time. The definition of better will depend on your particular situation and circumstances.

When I unknowingly began what would later become The 15 Minute Master system, better for me was survival. It was not planning out an action step in a systematic 15-minute time frame. It was simply enduring, as in, *I just have to get through the next 15 minutes.* I lived that way for a long time.

Eventually, I learned that better could mean more, so my favorite definition is that better means "more advantageous or effective."

Better is about positioning yourself in such a way that you can begin to solve a problem, making an advantageous move or decision to nudge the odds in your favor so the outcome will be acceptable, at the least. Giving yourself an advantage over a problem or issue is as simple as deciding on a course of action—or inaction—to manage it.

Which brings us to effective. Webster says "effective" means "producing a decided, decisive, or desired effect." I like those words. So much of life involves increasing and ever-changing variables. The thought that anything can be managed to produce a "decided, decisive, or desired" outcome almost makes my heart sing. You mean I can actually control something? Whaaaaaattt???!!!!

But wait, let's not get ahead of ourselves. The idea of control is a tricky devil. The word itself offers the promise of having everything handled, which is rarely the case, ever. Life simply contains too many variables for anything to be completely in our control. Yet we can break down any situation into manageable bites, giving us partial control of any process, even if that control simply manifests in mastery of our *reaction* to a problem, incident, or situation.

The 15 Minute Master dismantles problems brick by brick. One step at a time, making everything simple. Note the use of the word "simple." I didn't say "easy," I didn't say "fun." I said "simple." At its most basic, everything in life is simple. You either do something or you don't do it, and the result of that action or inaction leads to the next thing, which either adds to or helps solve a problem. Not necessarily easy, but simple.

The actions themselves may or may not be easy. That's almost beside the point. An action is just a thing you do that results in something. Even inaction is an action, as it results in something either happening or not happening. You're still left with a situation that will eventually resolve—everything does—whether you do anything or not. The point of acting is to try to resolve things in your favor. It won't always happen that way, but at least you've improved the odds by doing—or not doing—something. (I said it was tricky.)

At its most basic, everything in life is simple.

Not necessarily easy, but simple.

If you decide against acting because the action is hard or unpleasant, know that is a form of action as well; you're just taking your influence out of the equation and letting all the other variables have their way without your input. That may, in fact, be the best thing for you. Only you can make that call. But by implementing The 15 Minute Master, you'll give yourself the clarity to determine whether you want to do something or nothing, and at least you'll be able to understand, if not be happy about, the consequences.

At the same time, know that inaction may be the right choice to make a situation better. As humans, as problem-solvers, we tend toward thinking our actions or influence are sure to make things better, which is not always the case. Sometimes we need to butt out and let stuff resolve without our two cents. In that case, better means—stay out of it. (More on this later.)

Either way, "better" implies movement, and that's the goal of The 15 Minute Master. As a tool to help you get un-stuck, the process provides a step-by-step guide to empower you to figure out what "better" means to you. That will lead to movement in any situation. A plan, a clear course of action (one action, at least to start) will lead to something else—another step to be taken, another situation to be dealt with.

But "better" doesn't always mean forward movement. Life is a series of dance moves. You move forward, you move back, and sometimes you just stay in place, swaying from side to side, but not really going anywhere. (Think of how comforting swaying with a baby is. Standing in place is not always bad.) Better can vary, sometimes from week to week, day to day, or even hour to hour.

Life is a series of dance moves. You move forward, you move back, and sometimes you just stay in place, swaying from side to side.

There is a measure of subjectivity to "better," because sometimes you may need immediate relief from something, yet on another day, you may be stronger mentally, emotionally, physically, or spiritually to hold out for a different outcome, giving "better" a different definition on that day, and therefore, inspiring a different choice for your action step. Does this muddy the waters? A little. Yet spending time working The 15 Minute Master program will encourage you to take into consideration everything—facts, as well as subjective factors in your equation—to help you make the best determination for what "better" means to you in your circumstances, at your moment in time.

Forward movement, because we equate it to getting ahead, may be the ideal. And if there's anyone out there who always finds him/herself in the ideal circumstances to always propel forward movement, please call me; I must become your disciple. For most of us, though, life is a mix of the good, the bad, and at times, the downright ugly. When you find yourself smack in the middle of the ugly, forward isn't always possible. Sometimes, progress can simply mean maintaining the status quo, especially if variables don't allow for change.

Several years ago, my husband's mother suffered a traumatic brain injury causing her to need round-the-clock care. As of this writing, my husband and his siblings have managed to give his mother what she needs in her own home. It's been a challenge, to say the least, coming at great cost to us all (none so much as my mother-in-law, of course).

When we think of what needs to be done to continue Marie's care, we're not expecting much forward movement. Circumstances being what they are, we're just interested in keeping standing what often resembles a house of cards.

Sometimes, that's the most you can expect from "better." You might not move forward, but if an issue arises that threatens the delicate scaffolding you've managed to construct to make a challenging situation bearable, "better" can mean, "Let's see what we have to do to keep this train wreck on the rails." Even an ongoing disaster benefits from a little maintenance occasionally.

Similarly, "better" can also mean taking a step back. To continue with the example above, and as anyone caring for a loved one knows, sometimes you just need to step away to recharge. The need for a break arises in most long-term challenges and should never be seen as a defeat. However, it's more than acceptable to view it as a temporary retreat. Retreats allow you to replenish your depleted resources, indulge in some self-care, and return to the fight refreshed.

"Better" may also simply mean different. When in the midst of intense crisis, improvement may not always be possible, at least not in that moment. In those cases, "better" might mean a change of scenery, either mental or physical, to temporarily remove you from the situation, clear your head, or renew your energy to fight another hour. That's why hospitals have chapels and cafeterias (aside from the fact that doctors and nurses need nourishment, too). When it's all too much, you change the picture, do something different if only temporarily, and pray peacefully, or get yourself a snack—good courses of action whether you're in a hospital setting or not. If the most you can do in a moment is simply something different, that's your better; go for it.

Another word of caution: Better doesn't always mean good. Or happy, or fun. Sometimes making something better means walking farther into the fire so you can come closer to getting out on the other side. Sometimes, life just sucks. We all end up in those places. The question is, are you going to live there, or are you just visiting? Sometimes, to get to good, we must go through god-awful. The key is to move.

> Sometimes, life just sucks.
> We all end up in those places.
> The question is, are you going to live there,
> or are you just visiting?

I learned that lesson all too well when my son was in the throes of his active heroin addiction. I knew something was wrong so many times, but I couldn't bear to face the reality. So, I lived in the muck, keeping my family there with me, because I couldn't face the journey ahead. I knew it would be ugly, painful, and devastating. It wasn't until I realized that I was already in ugly, painful, and devastating, and would stay there indefinitely, allowing the rest of my family to suffer too, that I knew I had to move—farther into Hell. But it was the only way to get to the other side. In the words of the immortal Winston Churchill, "If you're going through Hell, keep going."

Making the decision to move farther into Hell was life-changing. Admitting that I was in WAY over my head, allowing experts to help with my son (in other words, getting him into rehab), was painful. But it was also a relief, one that I hadn't experienced while standing still in the mess. Use any cliché you like—ripping off the Band-Aid, jumping in the pool, taking your medicine—any way you slice it, sometimes we have to take on the yuck to get to the good stuff. And that requires that you DO something. That requires movement.

Movement, or change, is inevitable. Nothing, and I mean NOTHING, ever stays the same. The question becomes, if stuff is gonna be different, how do I influence it so it's better for me and those I care about? If you're lucky, movement will lead you to a happy, or at least happier, place. But when movement takes you farther into the muck, which may be necessary to come out on the other side, keep your eyes on the end-game. Sometimes things have to get worse before they get better.

I promise you, if you follow the guidelines of The 15 Minute Master, things will get better. Maybe not unicorns and rainbows better, at least not right away, but better. You'll have a plan, you'll have more control, or realize when you don't so you can back off. You'll move, and you'll have planned the movement in the direction you want to go. You'll discover that movement leads to opportunity—for improvement, or sometimes just for necessary change, which may be the answer you never knew you were looking for.

> You'll discover that movement leads to opportunity—for improvement, or sometimes just for necessary change, which may be the answer you never knew you were looking for.

Chapter 3
Who Does It Work For?

Who does the 15 Minute Master work for? (My apologies, grammar sticklers.) The short answer is anyone and everyone. The system is not rocket science. Far from it. Laid out in theory it couldn't be simpler: Set aside 15 minutes, concentrate on one issue or problem, develop at least one action step, and implement it. Followed and implemented, the system works.

More important is *why* the system works for everyone. People get stuck for all kinds of reasons—uncertainty, fear, procrastination, laziness, busyness, even youth and age are factors. Action can grind to a halt for many reasons, and The 15 Minute Master can address all of them.

We all have personality traits, not to mention our age, circumstances, etc. that keep us from acting, solving problems, achieving what we want to achieve, and becoming who we want to be. Once we identify what's keeping us stuck, we can address it and move forward. I'm a victim of a multitude of character flaws that have had me encased in a pair of cement shoes, creating excuse after excuse about why I couldn't get something done, why stuff was going wrong for me, blah, blah, blah, for what seemed like forever.

> We all have personality traits,
> not to mention our age, circumstances, etc.
> that keep us from acting, solving problems,
> achieving what we want to achieve,
> and becoming who we want to be.

Since the peculiarities of personality influence how we think, make decisions, and behave, it's helpful to figure out what you're bringing to the table and how your personality may react to The 15 Minute Master. Hopefully, you're willing to be honest in your personal assessment, because you're listed somewhere below. Maybe in several places. (My husband once told me it was impossible to get bored with me because he never knows which of my eight personalities he's going to encounter on any given day. Poor guy.)

I've had to do a ton of work to get out of my own way, but I finally have (most of the time), and I'd like to make it easier for you, too. You're somewhere in the following paragraphs, I know it. (I'm in a lot of them.) Read on, oh brave one, figure out who you are in the below, and let's do something about it together.

The Generational Divide

How old are you?

Forgive me for seeming impolite, but it's an important question. Our age, and where we fall in the generational divide, will affect how we approach and implement The 15 Minute Master.

So, the question then becomes, what does 15 minutes mean to you?

Easy enough. Fifteen minutes is one quarter of an hour, one half of a TV sitcom, one stop at Dunkin' as you scarf down your breakfast on the go. It's nothing, really. No time at all. It goes by in a flash, which is why I could manage my life in 15-minute bites when my son was in the throes of his addiction. Fifteen minutes, I could do.

But 15 minutes has become a generational concept. While it's no time at all to someone like me, who's past the half-century mark (ouch, that stings), to a millennial or younger, 15 minutes can seem like half a day. If you doubt me, ask a young person to put down their phone for 15 minutes. When you do, hand them a paper bag and make sure they breathe into it so they don't hyperventilate.

To a millennial, 15 minutes might be reading and sending 100 text messages, checking a work schedule for one of the three jobs they're forced to work as they haven't found a full-time position yet, trying to keep up with the newest technology, watching half a dozen videos while posting on Twitter, or chatting with someone on speaker phone. Actually, nix that last part; millennials never talk on the phone.

The concept of time has changed dramatically with the internet age. We have 24-hour news cycles, constant access to everyone we know through email, texts, and social media, and we can work all day, every day, which some of us have been forced to do. The result is a continual influx of information, changing circumstances and scattered attention spans.

Yet, regardless of where we fall on the age spectrum, The 15 Minute Master works, if we see 15 minutes as nothing at all, or as a training exercise in focus. Let's start with those of a "certain age…."

Old-Heads, Unite!

According to my kids, I'm an "Old Head," a.k.a., one who is, shall we say, golfing on the back nine. Our perception of time is that it flies—quickly—in fact, too fast for us to keep up, probably because we recognize that there's less ahead of us than there is behind us.

It's disconcerting, and it's exactly why 15 minutes seems like nothing, especially when what happened 15 years ago can seem like it was only yesterday. That's precisely why, when asked to focus on 15 minutes as part of the 15 Minute Master program, we Old Heads think, *15 minutes? No problem. I can do that.*

But we don't do it, because our concept of time can also work against us. We believe that 15 minutes is so short a time that we couldn't possibly accomplish anything meaningful within it. We devalue its significance as we watch it slip away, and then mourn as it disappears. We get so stuck in our own habits and negative mental monologues that we think, *Ah, what's the use? It's been that way for years* (whatever "it" happens to be). *It would take forever to change anything.* So, we don't even try.

Okay, that was depressing. But it doesn't have to be. As "experienced" individuals, we know how valuable time is, and we know how it slips through our fingers. Which is precisely why we should grab onto that 15-minute slot, squeeze out every valuable second, use it to get a grip on our stuff, and then move onto the next 15 minutes, in which we'll hopefully feel confident enough in what we've set in motion to have a glass of wine and chill for a little.

By claiming our time in the 15 Minute Master, we Old Heads can make the most of every moment, every thought, every decision, stripping issues down to their most basic and then dealing with them, using time intentionally instead of watching it sift through the hourglass. Instead of looking at 15 minutes as no time at all, no time to change anything, no time to do anything significant, we can view it as a challenge. What exactly can I do in 15 minutes? You'll be amazed by the answer.

The Millennial Conflict

Now for the millennials (anyone my kids' ages) and younger, who naturally disagree with just about everything I say. (Okay, that's just my kids, but conflict and differences between generations is hardly new ground.) Technology has dramatically changed our ideas about time, especially for those who can't remember a world without the internet. For this group, multi-tasking is a given. It's more like multi-multi-tasking, as noted in the aforementioned texting, job searching, technology training, tweeting, Instagram and Pinterest scouring.

Through no fault of their own, the younger set finds focus challenging, at best. With an incessant barrage of information, as well as changing rules on everything we oldsters knew to be true (work hard, do the right thing, and you'll land a great career—HA!) the millennials have to dance twice as fast as older generations did just to stand in place. Focus requires that attention be paid, and it's not easy to pay attention to one thing when you're juggling fifty things at one time.

The idea of concentrating on one single thing at a time is foreign to anyone under the age of thirty, or maybe even thirty-five. They can't do it without risking falling behind. Yet, while that ability to bounce between multiple endeavors may enable this demographic to seemingly accomplish a lot, when your mind is zinging around like a pinball, not much gets accomplished in depth. There's little major planning, and lots of reacting. Not to mention that in the online world, where much millennial attention is focused, everything seems important, while most of it is a lot of smoke and mirrors. How can you tell what deserves attention and what doesn't?

Making any meaningful progress in life requires thought, planning, and action based on both. It requires follow-through and follow-up, to ensure that what was started gets finished. In a world where an average of 6,000 new apps were released EVERY DAY in 2018, it's challenging for this group to focus on anything longer than a nanosecond, because anything they do set their eyes on is old news before they can blink.

Which is why millennials really, REALLY need The 15 Minute Master. While we Old Heads look at focusing for 15 minutes as a breeze, millennials look at it like waterboarding or some other form of torture banned by the Geneva Convention. (Look it up, kids.)

The ability to contemplate anything for any length of time, even as little as a minute, is becoming as lost an art as reading a map. Remember those? How would anyone under thirty ever get around if not for Google Maps or Waze?

Learning how to focus one's mental energy, plan, and find a potential solution to a problem are skills necessary to fully-functioning adulthood, but skills that have atrophied in the younger set. And lest we Old Heads let ourselves off the hook, we can also be consumed by FOMO (Fear of Missing Out), since we're convinced we're modern-day dinosaurs doomed to extinction if we don't at least try to keep up, which is wildly hard to do. Then, we end up chasing our giant dinosaur tails in a never-ending search for relevance, not focusing on anything at all.

The result of this endless mental ping pong is that most of us, old and young alike, are incapable of the concentration, focus and intention necessary to consistently solve problems, big, small or in-between.

That's one thing the generations have in common. Beyond that, there are other personality traits at work that cross generational boundaries and complicate our ability to get stuff done. Check out some below and see where you land. Then, we'll get to the solution, which is to train ourselves to focus on short periods of time, one starting point toward one decision, one action, one solution. The 15 Minute Master.

The Procrastinator

Clearly, I fit in here, because instead of writing to complete this section, I watched Michael Bublé and James Cordon do Carpool Karaoke for 15 minutes. (Hey, no judging—at least I stuck with the 15 minute thing. And it was Michael Bublé. Sue me.) So yeah, I procrastinate. Who doesn't these days, with so much distraction available at the tap of a button?

We're all *Gone with the Wind*'s Scarlett O'Hara, promising to "think about it tomorrow." (I'm a movie fan, too.) Problem is, tomorrow never comes, and if it does, the issue has compounded, become more complicated and so knotty that we're overwhelmed by the mere thought of dealing with it. So, guess what? We put it off until tomorrow. Again.

The 15 Minute Master gives The Procrastinator a short, manageable time frame in which to address a problem. It contains the issue, providing a finite framework for getting started, which is The Procrastinator's main problem. The Procrastinator puts things off for a variety of reasons, each unique to an individual, but all with common underlying themes: the task at hand overwhelms, is too hard, or will take too much time to complete.

When The Procrastinator commits to The 15 Minute Master, the time frame itself takes overwhelming off the table. You can't solve a major problem in 15 minutes. But you *can* get a start on it. Once you start with a single action, you begin to chip away at both overwhelming and hard. Yes, your action step may be hard, but that's where you have to put on your grown-up panties and just do it. The 15 Minute Master, worked correctly, will give you the plan, and the motivation to get moving. It takes away The Procrastinator's major objections to getting stuff done. No more excuses; just take one step.

The Worrier

Do you stew, obsess and worry over problems, real and imagined, like a dog working a bone? The Worrier takes a problem, big or small, and kneads it to death, creating and recreating possible scenarios, actions, outcomes, maybes, or might-bes until they're exhausted, stressed, and depleted, often by things that haven't happened yet and may never happen.

The Worrier wastes so much time making plans based on what-ifs, that they overlook or fail to act on the reality in front of them.

We all have a measure of The Worrier in us. It's the part that encourages us to formulate a plan of action. That alone would be great, except that The Worrier sees so many potential problems in almost every situation that they spend their life in problem-solving mode, rarely gaining enough clarity to institute a reasonable action aimed at solving an actual problem.

The 15 Minute Master forces The Worrier to get off the hamster wheel and stop spinning. By limiting the time The Worrier is "allowed" to spend thinking about an issue, the program helps The Worrier to contain the problem, and hopefully the worry. Creating a single action step that must be implemented before additional action takes place, further contains the what-ifs, as the action will change the situation in some way, thus changing the circumstances and possibly the problem itself.

The Worrier also tends to manufacture situations peripheral to the actual issue at hand, anticipating problems, predicting others' reactions, and complicating the path to clear action and solutions by creating alternate realities. The 15 Minute Master demands intense and limited focus, allowing for only one situation and one actionable step as a result of committing to the 15-minute time frame. Sticking with the plan encourages The Worrier to see only the facts of the situation, prompting action based on those, not imaginary plotlines crafted by a brain that should be writing fiction. (And yes, okay, this is me, too, but I don't write fiction. I write stuff telling everyone else what to do. Sorry, not sorry.)

It's time for The Worrier to get a grip—on problems, on reality, on possibilities. The 15 Minute Master is the tool to help.

The Control Freak

The Worrier has a sibling—The Control Freak. (and fine, this is me too. Yes, I've had a lot of therapy.) The Worrier often obsesses because s/he likes to be in control. Actually, "likes" is too kind a word; this type NEEDS to be in control. Having control over a situation is the only way The Worrier can sleep at night; thus, The Control Freak is born.

Like The Worrier, The Control Freak lives anticipating disaster. But instead of manifesting as worry, The Control Freak is self-deluding, convinced that if they anticipate all possible outcomes and then plan for them, insisting that things be done their way, they can keep unpleasant or truly terrible things from happening.

While annoying everyone around them, The Control Freak generally has good intentions. By taking over anything and everything, The Control Freak thinks they can ensure safety and well-being for themselves and their loved ones. It's a way to function by trying to guarantee certainty in a highly uncertain world.

By following through and asking/answering the questions posed in The 15 Minute Master, The Control Freak clarifies whether they have actual influence over a situation or whether they're simply trying to manipulate circumstances and variables to their liking, a.k.a. control stuff they have no business trying to control.

Once the realistic sphere of influence is determined, The 15 Minute Master provides a framework to help The Control Freak tame the urge to jump into everything by requiring that action be limited to one thing and one thing only, until the situation evolves. This is a pretty way of saying The 15 Minute Master gives The Control Freak boundaries, clarifying when it's time to butt out.

By defining what The Control Freak actually has control over—as opposed to endlessly butting into everyone else's business trying to grasp control—and setting up boundaries for action, The 15 Minute Master helps The Control Freak to rein it in, already. This makes them far less annoying (still talking about me, here) and helps to alleviate the stress they create for themselves by trying to be in charge of everybody's everything. Ahhhhhh…and everyone is happier!

The Scaredy-Cat

Fear. It's a primal human emotion. In fact, it's been said that all human interactions are based on love or fear. And while it would be wonderful to believe that love is our main motivation for action, most times, it's fear. Fear of failure, fear of loss, fear of change.

Enter The Scaredy-Cat. The Scaredy-Cat is afraid of just about everything, which of course includes making decisions and enforcing actions to address problems. Like The Procrastinator, The Scaredy-Cat won't or can't bring her/himself to get to it, for fear of any of the above. If Scaredy-Cats act, they believe they'll make the wrong choice, making a difficult situation worse or somehow screwing up a good one. The last thing The Scaredy-Cat wants is to be responsible for exacerbating or causing problems, because then someone might get mad at her/him, which may lead to yelling, which The Scaredy-Cat is afraid of. The Scaredy-Cat then ends up living in an uncomfortable state of inertia.

The Scaredy-Cat needs to be pushed into both making a decision and acting on it. By providing an opportunity for intense focus on a problem and allowing for options and choices to be reviewed before action takes place, The 15 Minute Master helps The Scaredy-Cat feel more prepared for what comes next, which is important to someone who is afraid of the future.

Once we stare an issue in the face, unblinking for 15 focused minutes (don't really not blink, that would hurt), we see more clearly the reality of what in the situation there is, or more importantly isn't, to be frightened of. Yes, the unknown is scary and unpredictable. But by examining the circumstances of a problem or issue, determining what's real and what's an imagined fear, The Scaredy-Cat can plan for likelihoods and ignore, or at least suppress, the what-ifs that frighten them.

While the fear won't entirely disappear, it can be managed or contained through preparation and awareness. The 15 Minute Master helps The Scaredy-Cat see the man behind the curtain for who he really is, exposing the Bogeyman as perhaps not so scary after all.

The Busy Bee

Busy, busy, busy! Everyone is so very busy, but none so much as The Busy Bee, who wears busyness like a badge of honor—and an excuse. The Busy Bee, being super busy, can avoid taking on unpleasant tasks, overwhelming tasks, and boring tasks, because they've just got so much else to do. But avoiding action just makes stuff harder in the long run, complicating issues, creating more problems, and prolonging the agony of just handling it, for heaven's sake.

The Busy Bee is busy for a lot of reasons—most times legitimate, sometimes manufactured. Because they're so darned busy, The Busy Bee tends to be reactive, instead of proactive, putting out fires as they ignite, living daily life in mini-crisis mode. As a result, The Busy Bee is often frazzled, stressed, and overwhelmed.

The 15 Minute Master helps The Busy Bee to get a grip on the busyness, providing a framework for determining what's legitimate busyness and what's manufactured. Why would anyone manufacture busyness? Sometimes The Busy Bee creates stuff to do to avoid the major yuck that life throws her/his way. It's much harder to hit a moving target, so flitting from item to item on a never-ending "To-Do" list gives The Busy Bee an excuse not to proactively address life's bigger messes, which usually means the messes just get bigger and messier.

By taking an unflinching look at the legitimacy of The Busy Bee's "To-Do" list, The 15 Minute Master holds The Busy Bee accountable to determine what's really in their power to control. It then offers the opportunity to prioritize and create a plan for getting stuff done, once and for all, as well as to carve out time for either relaxing (which The Busy Bee really, REALLY needs, but is always too busy for), or more busy stuff, which they're kind of addicted to. With continued practice and luck, though, The Busy Bee will finally enjoy the benefits of a little R & R and sit the heck down for once, because they need it, and they're driving the rest of us crazy.

Bottom line? You can use
the principles and format of
The 15 Minute Master to:

- Determine your place in a situation
- Stop stewing over every damn thing
- Decide on an action and do it, already
- Get your nose out of other people's business
- Quit being afraid of everything
- Stop using busyness as an excuse
- And finally, put on your grown-up panties and manage stuff in a timely, effective way

The solution is to train ourselves to focus on short periods of time, one starting point toward one solution, one decision, one action. The solution is The 15 Minute Master. So, let's get to it. It's time to help you make life better, 15 minutes at a time.

Chapter 4
The Set-Up

Your Physical Space

How do you solve problems? Each of the characters in the "Who Does It Work For" chapter solves problems in a different way, usually butting heads with their personality quirks so that problem solving becomes a problem itself.

The goal of The 15 Minute Master is to provide a simple framework useful for any personality. By keeping the process simple, we eliminate excuses. There's no grand scheme, forms you have to fill out, meetings you must attend, nor groups to join. Yet, in order for this method to reach optimal effectiveness, there is a certain amount of basic preparation that will help ensure a positive result.

So here goes: First, set aside 15 minutes: a solid 15-minute time frame when you can focus, uninterrupted, on the task at hand. Choose a time when you have some energy. For some of us that's first thing in the morning—before we're immersed in the minutiae of daily living. For others, it's at day's end, when one can reflect on what happened during the day in order to figure out how to plan for tomorrow. The time of day itself is irrelevant, provided it's a time when you feel capable of focus, your mind open enough to consider a few essential questions and uncluttered enough to manage some simple analysis. You're the best one to determine when, based on your lifestyle. Fifteen minutes, uninterrupted. That's where we start.

In order to be uninterrupted, you may want to address your general wants and desires before you begin. In other words, if you're like me, and the thought of food crosses your mind every 30 seconds, get a snack and feel free to nibble while working. Yes, it's probably best to maintain total focus, but I'm being a realist, here. If I'm not fed and watered regularly, nothing gets done. Nothing. So, get a glass of something (save the wine as a reward for when you're done), a little snack—not a full meal—and set it where you're going to work The 15 Minute Master—a table or desk, not the couch.

Let's return to the word, "uninterrupted." That means a quiet place. Remember quiet?

Quiet, in our constantly connected, buzzing, beeping, "hey, pay attention or you might miss something" world, is a rare commodity. As such, we must seek it out, and, if necessary, create it, by rigorously stripping our surroundings of the never-ending noise that calls for our attention. For The 15 Minute Master to work, you need to SILENCE your surroundings.

Remember quiet? We must seek it out, and, if necessary, create it, by rigorously stripping our surroundings of the never-ending noise that calls for our attention.

That means no TV, no music, NO CELL PHONE! Put it in a drawer, put it in the hamper, throw it out the window—I don't care what you do with it, but get it away from you for 15 solid, uninterrupted minutes. And I do not mean put the phone on buzz or beep, instead of ring, or whatever. I mean, get it out of the room. The world will continue to turn on its axis even if you don't answer the umpteenth call about how you can get a better interest rate on your credit card.

Minimize distractions—make sure the dog is out, the kids are at school or parked in front of some mind-numbing electronic device (no, I don't generally advocate this, but desperate times…), and don't even think about opening your email. If you must, use ear plugs, or earbuds (not connected to music), and put everyone on notice that for the next 15 minutes, you are unavailable, unless there's bloodshed or a zombie apocalypse.

Create, intentionally, the setting you need to accomplish something. Recall what you did when you had an important exam to pass. You went to the library, or locked yourself in your room, or just hid for a few hours so you could study. This is the same thing, just for a 15-minute period. Do whatever worked then—if not literally, then replicate the quiet however you can, in your physical surroundings.

Previously, I mentioned sitting at a table or desk, not a couch. The table is more important than it sounds. Our surroundings influence how we feel, how we think, and how we behave. To get the most out of The 15 Minute Master, choose a room where you feel comfortable and safe, but not so comfortable that you want to snuggle up with a blankie and a good book. Be sure there's good lighting; bright light, whether natural or artificial, can stimulate motivation and energy levels, staving off depression and anxiety. Further, sitting at a work desk or table, with a straight-backed chair, will put you in work mode, signaling your brain that it's time to get serious (plus, if you're slightly uncomfortable, you'll concentrate just to finish the job so you won't have to sit there too long).

Next, figure out how you want to record your progress. To keep a running log of your ideas and decisions, get yourself either a notebook (not just a piece of paper) or set up a document/folder/secret hiding place on your computer on which to work and keep your thoughts. However you choose to keep records and maintain documents, be certain your 15 Minute Master workbook or document is respected—by you. This is not a place to be your usual half-assed self and write everything down on Post-It notes (again, me here, but also possibly you).

If you're a tactile person and write stuff down the old-fashioned way, using pen and paper, treat yourself to a new notebook especially designed for use with The 15 Minute Master. Honor the fact that you're committing to this work and respect the time, the process, and your commitment by keeping track of your effort in a specially designated place. Not only will this keep your work on the program centrally located, it will enable you to see your progress as you continue to work the system over time. If what I think will happen actually happens (and it will), you'll notice increased clarity and focus in your approach to problems, as you cut through the crap faster and get to the heart of issues sooner.

You'll also figure out patterns of behavior, discovering your strengths and weaknesses. Then you can begin to anticipate challenges before they fully manifest, perhaps minimizing problems before they grow. You can also build your personal skill set while likewise recognizing when it's time to call in the cavalry before disaster strikes (not that that's ever happened to me).

If your laptop/desktop is your preference for work, you've got a little more prep to do—namely, close your email, Facebook, You Tube, shopping sites, and anything else on your search browser. In fact, if you can't trust yourself to ignore open sites, close your browser entirely. Work in Microsoft Office and save your work in your online programs for later. It's easy enough to think, *Oh it's only 15 minutes, I can focus for 15 minutes without looking at Facebook or YouTube.* But take it from one who has become a master at Spider Solitaire when I'm stuck for even a nanosecond on anything, it's all too easy to click over to a distraction when the work gets hard. And sometimes, this work is going to be hard.

All of this may seem like a lot of words to simply get you to sit down in a quiet place and focus. Yet the constant barrage of information, distraction, and general noise we face every day can make it impossible to focus on anything long enough to formulate, with intention, an action plan for anything. We often miss the value in creating a safe space, a place to think, to question, to formulate a plan. In order to get the most out of The 15 Minute Master, you need your safe, quiet space. When you don't need to think about where you are, you can think about what you're doing.

Your Mental Space

A physical setting is important, but even more important is the setting inside your head. Once you've created your quiet external space, you must quiet your internal space. Easier said than done, because even if you've physically removed distractions, the hamster in your head won't so easily be put off its urge to hop on its wheel and run. Once again, our wonderful, magical brains, capable of so much, don't naturally deal well with so little. If the external stimulation winds down, our brains are more than capable of filling in the gaps with mental lists of obligations or shoulds, memories, what-ifs, songs that have wormed their way into our ears...you name it.

> A physical setting is important, but even more important is the setting inside of your head. Once you've created your quiet external space, you must quiet your internal space.

So, set your mind. Prepare yourself mentally by giving yourself permission to make this work a priority—sans guilt. No feeling badly because someone has asked you to do something and you're putting it off, no guilt because you're not answering the phone when your mother is calling (which you won't hear anyway because your phone IS NOT NEAR YOU), no worrying about getting dinner started (they can eat a bowl of Cheerios; it won't kill them).

Clear mental space to focus on the task at hand. Given the sheer number of thoughts that cross our mind daily (some researchers estimate the number is 50,000-70,000!), quieting the mind for intentional focus is not only helpful, it's essential, and not easy. As anyone who meditates will tell you, the flow of information into our brains is constant. When you find yourself drifting, just call your mind back to the task at hand, without the usual scolding you give yourself when you don't get something right.

Feel free to SHUSH your brain. Recall what we instinctively do when a child is crying. We automatically make that comforting "Shhhhhhh" sound, in an effort to calm. Guess what? It still works, even on an adult brain. When getting in the mental mindset for The 15 Minute Master, shushing your brain is incredibly effective.

Not to get all New-Agey on you, but closing your eyes and taking some deep breaths once you're settled in your work space will calm your mind as well. Eyes closed, inhale to a slow count of four, hold your breath for a count of four, exhale to a count of four. A peaceful start to this process will encourage positive energy. (Okay, maybe a little New-Agey.) Prepping your mind for an intentional activity is an essential practice for success, and one we rarely do. Take a few minutes for a mental sweep of the junk in your head to make way for progress and clarity.

If you're going to give this process a shot, the preparation of your physical space, and your physical mind, is essential. Find your 15 minutes, your quiet place, your peaceful mind, and prepare to make things better.

Chapter 5
Creating the Framework

The First Two Minutes

Okay, we're ready. You've created a quiet space, calmed your mind, and given yourself permission to step away from your day for 15 uninterrupted minutes to make things better. We'll start by creating a framework for your issue, which will involve determining the exact problem, setting a boundary, a focus, and an intention. This is the beginning of The 15 Minute Master process. Set your timer for two minutes and begin with the first step, below. (Yes, I know I told you to put away your phone. Use a watch, a clock, your computer. You can figure this out.)

Is It Real?

Before addressing any problem, it's crucial to determine EXACTLY what the problem is. What are you really dealing with? Not the symptoms of the issue, the issue itself. You have to know what you're up against before attempting to tackle it. When in the midst of crisis, or any situation in which we don't know where to go, clarity is the place to start.

When addressing a problem, the most basic question is this: Is it real?

Is your problem a real thing? Is the situation currently unfolding in the present? Is something actually happening, or are you just making the whole thing up?

For better or worse, I am eminently qualified to force you to answer this question. I performed in a lot of plays in high school, and am a card-carrying member of the Drama Geeks Society. (Not a real thing, but if it were, I'd have been president, or queen, or something.) Even when I wasn't on stage, I was performing. I could turn running out of mayo for my sandwich into a scene worthy of a Tony award. I could cry on cue because I was always crying—don't get my mother started. In short, I was dramatic.

This was fine when I was a teenage drama queen. But as I got older, I found it difficult to leave my dramatics behind, resulting in copious amounts of time and energy wasted on problems of my own manufacturing, which weren't really problems until I made them so. Shame on me.

When life as a grown-up became more complicated, as it inevitably does, I found myself overwhelmed, suffering from panic attacks, high blood pressure, and depression, all while in my early thirties, trying to raise three little ones. It was ugly. *I* was ugly, making mountains out of molehills, piling stress on my marriage and family and manufacturing problems out of nothing more than life's everyday challenges and annoyances, all while trying to be perfect, which I decidedly was not.

It took a long time for me to get over myself. But when I did (lots of therapy and some awesome pharmaceuticals), I discovered that life was a lot more pleasant when I wasn't creating chaos out of nothing. I realized that punishing myself by creating angst was unnecessary, as life had enough punishment in store without my contributions. When I finally stopped creating imaginary problems, I had the strength, energy, and clarity to figure out what to do about some real ones—strength I needed for what was to come.

So, I ask you again: Is this a real problem, or a by-product of your over-active imagination? If it's real, The 15 Minute Master can help you move toward a solution. If it isn't, the program can also show you it's time to get out of your own damn way and stop sabotaging yourself. Real life is hard enough. Save the drama for binge-watching and don't make your reality any more complicated than it already is.

Boundaries

Have you ever heard the expression, "Good fences make good neighbors?" From the Robert Frost poem, "Mending Wall," the fence between properties is meant to keep everyone's business on their own side. To each his own; no mixing messes. There's a measure of order implied by a fence. It contains stuff; keeping things where they belong.

Problems and crises have a tendency to spill over, invading areas where they had no origin, yet affecting the periphery, nonetheless. Such issues create collateral damage, particularly if we allow them to fester and grow. Uncontained, a problem will have repercussions, rippling like a pebble in a pond, until the effects reach far beyond the source.

It's time to build a mental fence.

By setting aside a specific, contained time frame to examine an issue, we also establish a boundary for defining and containing the problem and then considering action. With a brief amount of time, it's essential to cut to the chase: What is the root issue, minus the offshoots that are beginning to grow and create trouble? It's easy to lose sight of the root—where the whole thing started, especially if "whatever this is" has been going on for a while. Yet setting up a boundary around the perimeter of a problem and homing in on the primary cause allows us to address specific courses of action aimed at the heart of the beast. Once you've addressed the main problem, the additional growths eventually wither and die.

Setting up a boundary around the perimeter of a problem and homing in on the primary cause allows us to address specific courses of action aimed at the heart of the beast.

I thought about being a doctor when I was little (before I took a chemistry class and decided, "Aw, hell no!"). But even at an early age, I could never figure out why anyone would take medicine to alleviate the symptoms of an illness without directly addressing the cause of an illness. Why temporarily treat a symptom when you could get rid of the whole problem once and for all by attacking the source? For example, while in college, I found myself with a crushing headache every time I left a particular class. I managed to get through by scarfing down tons of Tylenol. But it was only when I finished the course and eliminated the source of the problem—a pompous blowhard of a professor and course material wholly centered on James Joyce's *Ulysses* (waterboarding would have been less painful)—that I was finally free of the migraines.

The 15 Minute Master encourages us to dig into the source of the headache, define it and address it once and for all, instead of fussing around with the extraneous growths that have sprouted as a result of ignoring the main problem. Snipping the distracting offshoots, even though they may be the very things annoying us, only serves to prolong the challenges. With the source still functioning, the sneaky little buggers will just find another place to rear their ugly heads. Find the root, build a fence around it and attack it once and for all.

A friend of mine—I'll call her Cindy—met me for dinner recently. Even though her family is grown, Cindy told me that in answer to her daughter's plea, she made dinner for her husband and kids before she left to eat her own dinner out. After enjoying a wonderful time and parting ways, Cindy texted me later to say that she came home to find that no one cleaned up the kitchen! She cooked a meal she didn't eat, went out, and came home to a mess.

What's the problem here? Where do we set up the boundary and plan our attack? Sure, it's the messy kitchen, but that's the sneaky offshoot. The real issue is that Cindy's family expects her to be their maidservant—a role most moms play when their kids are young, certainly, but one that must be bravely surrendered when everyone is more than capable of making their own dinner.

Anyone can pitch a fit about a messy kitchen, but unless one contains and then zeroes in on the main issue—the fact that Cindy is slave labor in her own house—only the details are going to change here. Next time, it may not be a messy kitchen, but Cindy will find herself doing laundry at midnight or scrubbing toilets in bathrooms she doesn't use until she's shuffling around with a walker and lugging an oxygen tank.

Setting a boundary around an issue using The 15 Minute Master as a guide accomplishes two things. First, you identify and contain the real problem without getting lost in the undergrowth. Second, you create an action step using specific strategies intended to address that one particular situation. In time, you can address the other messes swirling around you, but setting up a boundary keeps attention on one thing, allowing you to focus and deal with the main issue once and for all.

Focus

But what about that word, "focus?" Building a fence, or setting any kind of boundary requires concentration, and with brains shuffling through upwards of 50,000 thoughts a day, focus is in short supply. Add to our internal chaos the massive amounts of information and distractions to come our way at any given moment—Squirrel!—and it's a wonder anything ever gets done.

I don't know about you, but by the end of a day I often feel like I've been assaulted. I'm overwhelmed, and my head has that fuzzy, almost buzzing feeling that accompanies too much screen time. I try to sign off my devices at a reasonable hour, but what if I miss something? What then? Will the world continue to function?

Will I continue to function? What if I don't find out everything right at the moment it happens? How can I solve my problems? How can I solve the world's problems? So much depends on me knowing everything all of the time! AAAAAHHHHH!!!

Does it? Does it really? Um, no. But we've convinced ourselves that an unceasing barrage of information is the only way we'll be able to stay in the game long enough to compete in a world ready to pass us by at every moment. Yet is this game one of any consequence? And does worrying about keeping up, giving everything a split second of attention instead of even a full minute, let alone fifteen, accomplish anything?

If you're constantly chasing your tail, never taking the time to focus on anything long enough to make a serious difference because you're too busy posting your latest inspirational quote accompanied by a picture you took or found on a free site that you spent time Googling, (sigh) you'll quickly find yourself benched by life. Because real life doesn't happen online. It happens in, well, real life, which requires that we get our heads out of our... let's say screens, and FOCUS on doing something real.

The boundary we set up around the issue at hand allows us to pinpoint the problem, and *focus*. In the words of Arthur Miller, "attention must be paid," to our challenges, to the world around us, to ourselves.

How many times were you admonished to "pay attention" as a child in school? Before the advent of the internet and instant communication, paying attention was a mental skill that adults knew needed to be developed to accomplish anything meaningful in life. Now, with Big Brother Google answering every question at the click of a key, paying attention, like knowing how to dial a rotary phone, is a lost art.

Even more distressing, we've confused focus with the far more cool-sounding, "multitasking." How could multitasking not be awesome? After all, it has the word "multi" in it, and everyone knows that we Americans like more, more, and still more. Anything that does more than one thing at a time just has to be better, right?

Not so fast. Writer Kendra Cherry, on the website *verywell mind*, notes that "some researchers suggest that multitasking can actually reduce productivity by as much as 40 percent." Forty percent? Are you kidding me? Add that to the 35 percent of the time that I'm goofing off, playing Spider Solitaire, throwing in a load of laundry because I'm sick of staring at a blank computer screen when I'm supposed to be writing, or Kon-Mari-ing my drawers, and I've dropped to 25 percent efficiency, which is actually higher than I thought I was, come to think of it.

We've all got more on our plates than any other previous generation. Plus, things happen at warp speed, which you no longer have to be a Syfy geek to know means really, really fast. All the more reason why The 15 Minute Master is the solution. Using a 15-minute time frame to intentionally focus, or pay attention to one issue, one circumstance, one situation, encourages more than a cursory look, inviting you to look at the details, where the devil himself lies.

But committing to focus is only part of the equation. In order to truly focus on how you're going to make your issue better, you have to let go.

This is where you leave the coulda, woulda, shouldas at the door. No revisiting what you might have done but didn't. No beating yourself up for missed opportunities. No playing out scenarios that would have been great if they'd only been based in reality, which they weren't, or you wouldn't be working The 15 Minute Master.

Leave the coulda, woulda, shouldas at the door!

Part of clearing your head, part of focus, is becoming open to new possibilities or courses of action, which you won't be if you're still hung up on what might have happened, "if only...". "If only" is a fairy tale, and we're not living in a Disney movie. (If only.) So drop it. It serves no purpose, and reliving all of the might-haves will only slow you down and prolong the agony.

Paying attention, examining, focusing, plus releasing what might have happened but didn't regarding the particulars of a situation, is not only more productive, but actually has a calming effect on the brain, allowing one to tune out distractions and get into the mental space most efficient at problem solving. When we focus on one thing, one step toward better, we become faster and more proficient. It's being "in the zone," where distractions fade, clarity increases, and mental acuity sharpens. Professional athletes strive to find the zone, likening it to a mental state where everything slows down, allowing them to focus on one thing— getting the job done.

With focus, the zone is available to anyone. It's a personal sweet spot where productivity increases, and we rise above the noise and clamor of the everyday. Amazing things are possible in the zone, and it's free; we just have to choose it. (One of my favorite examples of someone being in the zone and acting with instinctive focus and intention is Dale Lamoureux. You probably don't know his name, but you've likely seen him. Dale is the guy who folds Domino's pizza boxes in their commercials like a machine, turning out hundreds of boxes in minutes with laser-like precision. He's such fun to watch!)

Focus is necessary, but also a relief. Have you ever found yourself so immersed in one thing that you literally lose track of time? Allowing yourself to sink entirely into a single thing frees the mind from stress resulting from multiple distractions and problems, as well as requires you to be present and in the moment. Eliminating past worries or future what-ifs creates a safe place to attend to the here and now, laying a framework for getting stuff done, the whole point of focus.

So, this is where you get to focus and examine your issue. Let go of what you could have, would have, or should have done. Turn the issue over, poke and prod it, looking for clues, cracks, identifiers—anything that will help you to figure out what the heck is going on so you can manage it, diffuse it, solve it (eventually). In other words, simply get on track toward addressing it. Focus, find your zone, and prepare to set your intention.

Intention

Focus is essential, but by itself, it can be misguided, especially if one focuses on the negative. That brings us to intention, which I thought was a bunch of hooey for a very long time.

Do you remember the book, *The Secret*? Upon first hearing of and then reading the book, I thought, *What a bunch of crap. All you have to do is set an intention and think about what you want and it magically appears! Yeah, sign me up.* I was practically insulted by the promise of the power of intention to manifest (another word that made me cringe) my dreams and desires. I spent so much time scoffing at the idea that we can create our reality that I refused to even consider that there might be an element of truth, or at least possibility, to it.

Okay, I suppose you need to hear me say it: I was wrong. I won't go so far as to say I'm a card-carrying member of the wish for it, blink like a genie, and watch it appear club, but I have become convinced that we attract what we think about. We become what we think we are.

I've always been a believer in the proverb, "God helps those who help themselves." My parents, particularly my father, firmly believed that no one was going to hand him anything. To his mind, life was all hard work and sweat, with a healthy heaping of suspicion and misery thrown in for good measure. Dad expected that anything he got in the world would require a gargantuan effort on his part. And even then, he figured he might not get what he wanted because he believed the powers that be were generally out to get him.

It didn't make for a particularly sunny vibe around our house, but it did give us all a great work ethic. Hence my conviction that I had to do for myself if God was going to give me any kind of a hand up, which I never expected anyway. An abundance mindset was NOT part of my upbringing. My dad believed that there was only so much good stuff to go around, and usually, it went to those lucky bastards (his term of endearment) who were on some kind of an inside track.

And that's how it usually went for him. It was what he expected; it was what he got.

It was also what I got, for a very long time. I expected things to be hard. They were. I expected to not get what I wanted. I didn't. I complained that things didn't go my way. They didn't. I rolled my eyes and huffed in exasperation at my poor husband, who was trying mightily to train his mind to be open to the possible, instead of closed to all possibilities.

The idea of creating our reality, of manifesting our dreams, seemed like nothing more than magical thinking. And without some sort of effort, it is. You can't magically create, with a wave of your hand and a proclamation, your dream life. You can't vanquish problems by wishing them away. However, by setting an intention that squarely faces the direction you want to go, you can create an environment that will focus your mind on how to get there, and ultimately get what you want, or something even better.

Set an intention that squarely faces the direction you want to go, and you can create an environment that will focus your mind on how to get there.

Yeah, yeah, I never believed it either. That is, until one evening, when I realized with a cosmic bang that I was manifesting exactly what I was putting out into the universe.

Dave and I were at a concert, sitting in the middle of a row of cramped theater seats. Much as I love the theater, it's hardly news that seating in those venues is designed for maximum dollars. Translation—you're forced to cram you bum into a seat designed for the butt of a three-year-old. A row with fifty seats should reasonably only have room for half that amount, but that means half the dollars, so squished bums be damned! No one is comfortable in theater seating. You tolerate it because you want to see the event.

The show was about to begin, but the seat next to me had remained empty. *Ah, I thought, a little extra room! This is gonna be great!* Then, because heaven forbid I embrace a positive thought, I immediately followed with, *Oh, who am I kidding? Any second now, a very large human is going to have to squeeze him/herself into this itty-bitty seat, and we're both going to be miserable.* Surprise! That's exactly what happened. Exactly. A very big fellow crammed himself into the seat while I moved as far over as possible, trying to give us both a little extra breathing room, to no avail. We both looked at each other, sighed, shrugged, and got on with it, yes, enjoying the show, but secretly cursing the sadist who designed the seats.

It wasn't until later, after I finished my grousing, that I realized I had created exactly what I'd been dreading. Not only that, I richly deserved the bad mood that followed. I'd all but asked for it, designing what would make me unhappy in my head and then expecting it to show up. Which it did, to the letter.

It was as though God reached down and bitch-slapped me. (Please let me apologize to the gentleman who was forced into making my nightmare a reality, so God could prove a point.) To this day, I firmly believe I was receiving a message, in no uncertain terms, to cut the crap and start pulling the good stuff toward me instead of the bad.

I'm blessed to know an amazing thought-leader and all-around wonderful man, named Bob Burg. Bob, along with his writing partner, John David Mann, is the author of the *Go-Giver* series of books, focused on the concept of giving and service as the best ways to influence, serve, and ultimately succeed in life and business. My co-hosts and I were lucky enough to have interviewed Bob on 4 Chicks Chatting, a podcast we created to engage, excite, and empower women. One of the things Bob talked about in that interview was "pull," as in the way we pull things to ourselves by our intention and actions.

Having experienced the "pull" concept so directly in that theater, and, after reflection, having experienced it in many, many ways throughout my life, I'm a believer. Our intentions get the ball rolling for us to start "pulling" results toward us—good, bad, or a mix of both. Why not pull the good stuff? Why not pull the best outcome, or at least set an intention for good?

Does "pulling" make it so? Of course not. Yet, setting the intention for a positive result to your current struggle at least puts you on the path of thinking about how to address your issues. It enables you to plan a course of action that points toward an outcome you desire, as opposed to assuming everything just sucks and will continue to do so no matter how you react.

Regardless of how your issues play out, and it won't be all sunshine and rainbows, expecting caca at every turn is a lousy way to look at life. Far better to expect something positive, set your mind and actions toward that result, and behave as though you deserve things to go well, which you do. Even if you don't get the brass ring, a mind set with positive intention allows you to see and be open to other opportunities, ones that may indirectly influence your current situation, or set you on a path toward a major shift, which may have been the answer all along.

I'm a believer thanks to experience, and not just because of the theater incident. Back in 2010, when I learned of my son's heroin addiction, I found myself in the middle of a perfect storm of life events in addition to David's drug problem (by far the most serious, of course). The economy was tanking, threatening our family business, the internet was changing the face of publishing, and my newspaper writing jobs were disappearing like dinosaurs hit by a meteor. Plus, I was approaching a birthday that mentally had me hunched over and breathing into a paper bag. It was ugly, with not even a pinprick of light at the end of the tunnel.

Drowning, with just the tip of my nose above water, I found myself lamenting to a friend one day about all of it. When the aging thing came up, I said, "Ugh. I'm SO not ready for granny panties!" And just like that, there was my pinprick of light. I had no idea what I would do with it, but at that moment, I decided that phrase would be a leaping off point for me. I set an intention to do something with those words, although I had no idea what form it would take.

After much thought, hard work, and 15 Minute Master sessions with myself, that intention became a blog, which became books, which became a speaking career, which became training and development programs…. None of it, not a single thing, was planned before the moment of intention. There was no reason to plan, because I didn't know what the heck I was planning for or about. I only knew that I had to move, that I had to do *something*, aside from wallow in my muck. I set the intention that I would get off my butt, stop complaining, and start to pull something good toward me, instead of trying so desperately to push the ugly away.

That single decision, that setting of the intention to make something work, despite the fact that I didn't know what or how, began to focus my mind on possibilities, instead of on lack. And that, my friends, made all the difference.

Now, while you're at it, set an intention to be patient throughout the 15 Minute Master process. When I decide to do something, I generally want it done yesterday; patience is not my strong suit. Given our culture's need to do and have everything faster, I'd guess patience isn't a strong suit for most of us. But it's exactly what's required for working through most problems and arriving at a reasonable outcome, especially given that every action initiated will likely result in something else happening to change the parameters of the situation. Making things BETTER, not immediately solving every life problem in an instant, is like a chess game. Moves will be made by you and others. Things will take time to play out—have patience.

Perhaps more important, be patient with yourself and your ability to "get it right" immediately. Although simplicity is the key with The 15 Minute Master, I'll say it again: simple doesn't always mean easy. The 15 Minute Master is, for all intents and purposes, a new habit, a new way of thinking, a new pattern of behavior for anyone. Simple as it is, it will take a little time for you to train your brain to focus and cut to the chase in order to move forward and to utilize the program efficiently. Be gentle with yourself and keep at it. It won't take long before you'll find yourself asking the three essential questions automatically when a new situation lands in your lap. It's worth the time and effort—I promise.

The Framework

The preceding sections on identifying the problem, setting up boundaries, developing focus, and setting an intention take longer than two minutes to read, no doubt. But once you get the concepts in your mind, the initial two-minute framework for beginning The 15 Minute Master process is simple and looks like this:

1. **Considering the problem:** Is the problem real? Yes, or no?

2. **Setting the Boundary:** Isolate the main problem and forget the offshoots.

3. **Setting the Focus:** Get into the focus zone, releasing coulda, woulda, shouldas.

4. **Setting the Intention:** Decide that things will get BETTER (not necessarily solved) and set the intention to pull positive energy toward you.

The framework sets the stage for your action. Put a pin in your problem, keep it still, focus the magnifying glass on it, and decide what result you want. You'll clear the way, at least far enough to start, which is what the 15 Minute Master is all about. Once you've begun, it's one foot in front of the other, one action following the previous one. Before you know it, you're looking in your rearview mirror at the mess behind you, waving buh-bye as you head toward your rainbow.

Now, let's get to the meat of the matter....

Chapter 6
The Three Questions

In 1984, Wendy's hamburger chain introduced a hilarious series of commercials featuring character actress, Clara Peller, asking, "Where's the beef?!" The 15 Minute Master has nothing to do with burgers (although I'm kind of hungry—shocking), but it's time we get to the beef, so here it is....

The heart of The 15 Minute Master lies in three simple questions. Three questions, asked in a certain order, which, when answered honestly, thoughtfully, and with focus, will lead you to a plan of action, or inaction (more later), for any situation.

In keeping with our theme, the questions are simple, but that doesn't mean the action steps resulting from your honest, focused answers will be easy. To reiterate, life is actually quite simple: you do something, or you don't. But as anyone who has ever lived knows, it ain't easy.

Each action, or lack thereof, will contribute to another action or reaction, depending upon the specifics of the situation. I'm no scientist, but I'm pretty sure there's a law of physics at work in there somewhere. This plays on until the situation is resolved in some way, and that rarely, if ever, happens immediately, or even quickly. But at the very least, taking some kind of action (or not), puts a measure of control back into your hands. That's price-less—and proactive—in a world where things appear to change exponentially every day.

Once you get started, The 15 Minute Master becomes a simple process of re-evaluating where you are with your issues and challenges as situations evolve and change. After you've answered your three questions with focus and intention, after you've initiated your action (or not) step, after you see what results from that, you simply go back and repeat the three-question process with the new information that resulted from your prior examination of that event. This is not rocket science. It's a simple process, repeated over and over, for just about any circumstance, that will lead you to an action plan and results.

The three questions are simple but absorbing. You can get lost within them, since posing each question will naturally give rise to other questions as you clarify your answers. The time allowed for each, including the framework setup, is suggested and can be altered as you become more comfortable with the program, but try to stick with the recommended suggestions at first. Once you get accustomed to the program and become familiar with the format, you'll be able to divide your time where it best suits you, spending more time where necessary, depending on each situation.

One of the most valuable outcomes of The 15 Minute Master is the opportunity to contain your thought processes and the amount of time spent ruminating on "stuff" without coming up with a plan. Set a timer when you begin. When you've spent the allotted time on a question, move on to the next one. The forced time constraint will eventually help you to focus, confining your wandering mind and making the process more efficient and consequently, effective.

At each phase of the process, read your answers aloud. Pay attention to how your responses sound coming out of your mouth. It seems silly, but if something doesn't sound right, it likely isn't. Mind your gut. Instinctive feelings about things should *never* be ignored. If it don't feel right, it probably ain't right.

Mind your gut. Instinctive feelings about things should *never* be ignored. If it don't feel right, it probably ain't right.

Remember, the goal is ONE ACTION STEP. One step, not a plan to solve an entire problem. Any issue, any thought, even one as simple as, *Should I go to the dry cleaners now or later?* will have some ramifications, some effect on whatever follows. Consequently, while you may be able to determine what *might* happen if you go to the dry cleaners now versus later, you won't have the *certainty* of that knowledge. So don't expect to have a reasonable idea of what might happen when dealing with larger issues; don't even try to figure it out. This plan is about looking at your one issue, answering the three questions, and coming up with *one single thing* to move you forward to make things better.

A word of caution: when you read the three questions, don't be put off by their simplicity and directness. It's easy to dismiss simple. In the United States, we still operate under the Puritanical notion that if something is worthwhile, it has to be hard. We must sweat and work and suffer through life in order to be worthy of any measure of success or happiness. Well, no it doesn't, and no we don't. The direct path to anything is a straight line. So it is with The 15 Minute Master. Simple, straightforward questions leading to simple, straightforward answers leading to simple (not necessarily EASY), straightforward actions that we do (or don't do). Sure, life is complicated, but again, we either do something or we don't, and that's pretty much the only place to start to unknot our challenges.

Okay, enough yammering. Here we go with question number one....

Chapter 7
Question #1:
What CAN I Do?

The Next Five Minutes

See? I told you it was simple. Simple, but not necessarily easy. Read the question again, aloud and slowly. Now do the same thing, but put the emphasis on the word "can." What **CAN** I do?

According to Dictionary.com, the word "can" means the following:

- To be able to; have the ability, power, or skill to
- To know how to
- To have the power or means to

What's unwritten here, and essential for our purposes, is having the words, "do something" follow each of the definitions above.

- To be able to; have the ability, power, or skill to DO SOMETHING

- To know how to DO SOMETHING
- To have the power or means to DO SOMETHING

In order to affect any kind of change whatsoever, one must be able to, have the ability to, have the power or skill to, know how to, or have the means to DO SOMETHING. Otherwise, the "can" quickly turns into a "can't."

Notice also that the question at hand is, "What CAN I do?" not, "What do I WANT to do?" We always WANT to fix a problem. We WANT to find a solution, or at least take some action. But wanting to do something and being able to do something are sometimes—especially in challenging circumstances—two different things.

Doing what we WANT to do is not always, or hardly ever, possible. If it were, our problems would melt and disappear like snowflakes, with little effort from us. We'd wave a magic wand and watch difficulties vanish as we skipped merrily through our days, rich, happy and problem-free.

Life isn't like that. Spending too much time thinking about what you WANT to do, as opposed to what you CAN do, means a lot of wasted time spent talking to yourself and creating a fantasy. When you finally snap out of it, you're still saddled with exactly what you were dealing with in the first place, and no further along in the process of reaching a solution.

Yet the question of what you want is not irrelevant. In fact, it's really where you should start, provided what you're focused on is not some fantastical result like making the problem disappear. (That's what we all want; it's just not possible.) Rather, what is it that you want that you can have some reasonable hope of attaining, based on what we CAN do? Put another way, what's your goal?

If you're anything like me, the word "goal" can make you hyperventilate and break out in hives. There's not a four-letter word in my vocabulary that inspires more angst in my brain. It smacks of New Year's resolutions unmet, cheerleading motivational speakers shouting me on, and the half-gallon of ice cream I dig my spoon into when I drop the ball once again.

Yet a goal is simply a result, the end-game, the closure to a situation. A goal is a win, or, in some situations, the least painful of the losses that may be an unfortunate inevitably. A goal is an outcome, and over that, we always have some influence, even if it's only to control our reaction to what's going on around us. A goal may also be as simple as a direction, a choice of movement. It needn't be lofty or extreme. Do I go left, do I go right, or do I stay put?

If a goal is a win, a good outcome, or at best the least painful one, then the question of what we WANT can be almost universally answered: We WANT the best for ourselves and our loved ones, in any and every situation, though that's a goal that's never completely attainable given the always-changing variables of life.

That's where the "BETTER" part comes in. If we can't get the best every single time, how do we at least make things better in this particular situation? And that brings us back to the question at hand: What CAN I do? What can I do to make this better?

This is where your list of variables comes in. What you CAN do will be based on a number of factors, namely:

- What is within my power?
- What skills do I have to address this?

- What resources can I bring to this?
- What is my level of control?

Sit down with your chosen form of recording your work (laptop, pen/paper, voice recorder), and ask yourself: What CAN I do here? What is within the realm of the possible, within my power? What am I able to do here to make this situation BETTER? What action can I take to improve things? Brainstorm, write down everything that comes to mind, and consider the factors below.

What you CAN do will have answers both factual and subjective. Your issue will have options that are actually possible, but don't forget another essential consideration: your energy level. How much energy do you have available to devote to this RIGHT NOW?

During my son's heroin addiction, my energy level was often minimal, if not non-existent. Consequently, my choices for action were sometimes limited by the fact that I was depleted. In evaluating action steps, I was sometimes just too tired to deal with the situation at hand in any major way. In determining what I could do, I had to factor myself into the equation. While certain steps might have been "better" in moving toward a significant solution, sometimes I simply had to choose the option that required the least of me at that time, knowing that on another occasion I'd be stronger and could react and behave differently.

That's okay.

We absolutely must take into account where we are in terms of circumstances when deciding what we CAN do in a situation. Self-awareness and a measure of self-care, or even self-preservation, should rightfully influence your decisions about future actions. You can always revisit the situation, tweak your action step or go in a completely different direction when you feel up to it. Do not discount your energy level. If you initiate an action when you don't have the energy to see it through, your result will almost certainly fall short of your goal. Be active, be thoughtful, but be realistic and even kind to yourself.

Depending on the specifics, the choices for action will vary. The most important thing: DO NOT TRY TO SOLVE THE ENTIRE PROBLEM. The question, "What can I do?" should be answered with one simple step that leads toward the overall goal. A singular action step to initiate movement toward the desired outcome is not only the simplest way to proceed, most often, it's the only way to proceed for one obvious reason: other stuff. Other stuff may be other people, other circumstances, or whatever "other" variable plays into your particular situation at any given moment.

"Other stuff" is the one constant in almost every instance, mainly because none of us lives on an island in complete self-sufficiency. We interact with others, depend on others, and take part in experiences involving others—and consequently, their stuff—all of the time. It is this "other stuff" that keeps us from having complete control over anything, and therefore limits the influence of our actions. What we do, unless it takes place in total isolation from "other stuff," will be influenced in some way by that stuff, requiring us to make our subsequent moves based on information we don't have in entirety or certainty when we're initiating a plan.

Put another way, you can only make one chess move at a time, until the other guy responds with a move of his own. Sure, you can prepare for what he *might* do. But until he takes his finger off the piece, you just don't know, which makes over-preparing for what might come next impractical at best, a total waste of time and energy at worst.

Which is not to say you plan your course of action with little thought to what comes next. Consider what might happen as a result of your actions and have an idea of what you might do in response. Just don't assume that you can map out every detail of a solution.

The point is to focus on ONE thing. A singular step, action, decision that you make that is within the realm of what you CAN actually and reasonably do to make a situation better.

The fact that it's one thing does not mean that thing will be easy. The fact that it's one thing means that it's simple. There's that truth again: Doing or not doing a thing is the simple fact. But easy? The thing in question is usually not.

Sometimes, your choice of action is between something easy and something hard. The key to making the decision as to which action to take is relative and personal. What's most important to you? Getting there quickly? Getting there painlessly? Getting there ASAP regardless of the cost? (I would not recommend the last option.) The answers to those questions will help you determine which of your CANs is the right one for your action step.

Remember the well-worn and time-tested clichés we all know and hate. Short term pain, long term gain. No pain, no gain. Yes, there is a pattern, one that will likely involve at least a smidgeon of discomfort. Most things we find ourselves debating internally will involve some sort of yuck from which we have to extricate ourselves. Not everything, but a lot. This explains why we're debating our course of action in the first place. If the solution were easy or fun, no problem. But when our options include how long is this gonna take, yuck, or ouch, well, that's when things get complicated.

But clichés are clichés because there is usually a kernel of truth contained within them. It's worth recalling another saying about pain here, "Wisdom is nothing more than healed pain." (Robert Gary Lee—Brown University.) Pain and discomfort are teachers. We learn when we suffer. I'm not advising that you put on a hair shirt and beat yourself regularly, but sometimes, doing what hurts is the only way to get through. Knowing this won't make it hurt less, but challenging experiences are the ones that make us better, stronger, wiser. So, it's time to put on your grown-up panties and DECIDE ALREADY.

What CAN you do? What is going to make your life/situation better because the action you've chosen brings you one step closer to solving a problem, addressing a need, finding peace, or whatever else you've decided is your priority? Recalling that better doesn't mean solved, what brings you closer to getting there, wherever "there" is? What one thing is within your means, power, ability to do that will make this better? Not necessarily fixed, over, resolved, but moving toward that end? What action is proactive?

Make your list, considering the above. Once you've recorded the possibilities of what you can do based upon your ability, skill, resources, energy, etc., you'll have a clear idea of how to proceed. But wait! Just because you CAN do something, just because it's within your power to act, it doesn't necessarily follow that you should. And that brings us to our next question....

Chapter 8
Question #2:
What SHOULD I Do?

The Next Five Minutes

So, you've got this problem, or situation, and you know you can do something about it. You know you can influence what's happening by speaking up, or pulling some strings, or otherwise inserting yourself into what's going on. Maybe jumping into the middle of it will even make you look better, like some kind of savior or something....

AAAAAHHHHHH!!! How many times (and there have been many) have I gotten myself involved in something and taken action when I simply shouldn't have? I can't even begin to answer as to a number. What I can say is that inserting myself when my best bet was to stay out of it always resulted in more complications, pain, and stress than if I'd just kept my mouth shut and didn't do anything. Sigh.

"Should" and "Shouldn't" are dangerous words, as noted in my book *Not Ready for Granny Panties*, where the tenth "commandment" reads, "Thou Shalt Stop 'Shoulding' Thyself." In many cases, we "should" ourselves through obligation—I *should* be working, I *should* clean the bathroom, I *should* mow the lawn, I *should* call my sister-in-law, etc. Conversely, we "shouldn't" ourselves as a form of self-denial—I *shouldn't* eat that ice cream, I *shouldn't* buy those shoes, I *shouldn't* be playing Candy Crush on my phone…and so on.

Ideally, everything we "should" do would benefit us, just as everything we "shouldn't" do would harm us. But in actuality, many of us have perverted the concept. For the purposes of The 15 Minute Master, however, you'll follow that rather simple statement—with a few caveats designed to determine if you should step into the pool in the first place.

The basic answer to the question "What SHOULD I do?" is something or nothing. But determining that you "should" act is a decision that must be made based on a number of factors:

- Is this my problem?
- How does this affect me?
- Is this any of my business?
- Will acting make things better?
- Will not acting make things better?

One of the most obvious, yet challenging questions to look squarely in the face is, "Is this my problem?" As social creatures, we constantly find ourselves immersed in things that concern us but are not totally "owned" by us. We might be involved, but peripherally, yet any involvement is often enough to get us spinning our wheels to fix or solve whatever is going on, whether fixing it is in our power, or even our responsibility. Good hearted souls that we are, we want to make things better. Yes, this is one of the goals of The 15 Minute Master, but only if we can do so without miring ourselves in the quicksand of things that we don't own, and are therefore not our problem, nor within our ability to resolve.

But, there's something about "helping" that appeals to us. We feel benevolent when we help, as if we're accessing our higher selves. Sometimes, that's true. But often, our "helping" people is an excuse. An excuse to not deal with our own stuff. An excuse to exert control over someone else, either because we want to be the boss of everyone and everything, or because we have no clue about how to handle our own lives, so we'll just try to run everyone else's. In the words of my favorite writer, the funny, honest and oh, so right Anne Lamott, "Help is the sunny side of control." (Oh Anne, why didn't I know you when I decided so many times in the past that I was going to play God?)

Help can be messy; know that going in. More important, know your motivation. Why are you getting involved? Why are you acting? Will this benefit you? Does it even concern you? If you are getting involved, is it because you just can't deal with your own mess right now and claiming this as your own allows you to avoid handling your issues while looking good? (Oh my, that's a powerful one.) Will your actions move things toward resolution or add fuel to the fire? Why, oh why, oh why, are you about to jump into this?

The only good reason to help is if the issue affects you directly, or at least impacts your life enough to warrant action. Are you being harmed? Held back from something you want or deserve? Prevented from achieving goals? Stuck in an ugly situation that's causing you stress? All reasons to act. Also legitimate—a loved one is being harmed, you feel strongly about a cause in which someone else is being harmed, or you see an injustice. All involve a singular leaning toward doing some good. If you are affected by an issue strongly enough to want to act, you have reason to explore your options.

So, ask the question aloud, emphasizing the word "should." What **SHOULD** I do?

If you're being honest with yourself, this question will be followed immediately by others, the first of which should be, "Is this any of my business?" Often, we feel that where our loved ones are concerned, problems are always our business, especially if we can "help." It pays to recall that our idea of a problem, as well as our idea of help, may not be the same as everyone else's.

I've told the story before of my South Philadelphia cousin, Valentina Bartolomeo (yes, that's her real name), who famously told my mother to "Mind your own business!" just before my mother took Valli to task for smoking. Note that Valli wasn't being offensive, either as she was smoking or in telling my mom to keep her nose (figuratively and literally) out of it. South Philly Italians equate such talk to a loving smack on the head, much like a mother bear will swat her cub to keep it out of trouble. With that one phrase, Valli squashed a potential argument. Yes, smoking is bad for you. Yes, Valli is part of our family and my mother doesn't want harm to come to her. But policing her cousin's behavior wasn't my mother's job. So while we may think it's our problem when a loved one is clearly doing something harmful, it might not be any of our business.

In deciding if you should act on any situation, always, ALWAYS ask yourself if it's any of your business. Be honest, because again, we *can* influence many situations, but it may not be our place to do so. If it isn't (though if you're anything like me, you know that if everyone would just listen to you, for god's sake, they wouldn't have these problems), STAY OUT OF IT. Again, as the wonderful Anne Lamott says, "Don't get your help and goodness all over everybody."

This isn't to say that you never help, especially when someone truly needs it. What it means is that you don't insert yourself into anyone else's business with the intention of solving their problems. Because—news flash—you won't. Unless it's an entirely self-contained situation—a neighbor needs a kid picked up from a practice, the same neighbor needs a cup of sugar, or that needy neighbor needs you to bring in the mail while she's on vacation—don't get involved. In fact, if you have a neighbor like that, there's a bigger problem—the neighbor doesn't have a clue how to manage her own life—and you should stay out of that as well.

Inserting yourself into others' lives is best, and only, done when you ask permission and set firm boundaries. It's far too easy to look at someone else's mess, and, if you're me, assume that, *Well, if I help them with this, then maybe they'll do that, and things will get better.* If that thought, or anything remotely like it, enters your mind when deciding if you SHOULD do something, the answer is, NO! Never, ever, ever get involved in a situation where other people are concerned that doesn't have a firm beginning and end. Otherwise, you will find yourself sucked into a rabbit hole from which you will only extricate yourself with great effort, wailing and gnashing of teeth. (If it sounds like I'm speaking from experience, I am.) "Mind your own business." It's a phrase I keep close to my heart and brain before I do just about anything.

Further, when answering the "What should I do?" question, be certain you aren't taking action because you're "offended." Without the possibility of some harm befalling you or someone else, it's a safe bet that you can, and should, stay out of it. If you're annoyed by something, don't like something, or something is driving you crazy, unless there's a longer-term consequence or the thorn is harming you or someone else, pull it out by refusing to be offended. You will always find a reason to be offended if you look for it. Don't look.

Few things are more colossal time-wasters or energy sucks than the minor annoyances we give space to in our heads. (I've spent way too much time clucking over old men who comb over the remaining six hairs on their heads and grow them into a ponytail.) Most times, these things are none of your business, or mine. Even small things, if we let them multiply, drain our brains of energy and time better spent on things that matter. The 15 Minute Master is designed to handle things that matter. Unfortunately, too many of us waste time on stuff that doesn't.

Realizing that is also one of the gifts The 15 Minute Master will give you if you find yourself repeatedly answering the "What should I do?" question with "Nothing, because it's none of my business." The 15 Minute Master will help you to determine if a situation is, in fact YOUR problem. Again, no one lives in a complete vacuum; we're all influenced by other stuff, other people, and changing circumstances. But sitting with the question, "What should I do?" for at least five minutes is a remarkable tool for clarifying what's your problem, what isn't, and exactly what is within your sphere of influence.

In truth, I've found few things more satisfying than proclaiming, "That's not my problem." It's as though a weight has been lifted from my shoulders. Ah, freedom! Boldly asserting that you're not responsible for something is freeing. (Some might say it's also a little bitchy, but I'm okay with that.) The space cleared in your brain when you release yourself from stuff that isn't your business, has little effect on you, or just isn't worth your time, can be filled with all manner of productive stuff—or a *Say Yes to the Dress* marathon. (Yeah, I'm still obsessed.) Freedom is freedom. What you do with it is YOUR business.

Few things are more satisfying than proclaiming, "That's NOT my problem."

Finally, recall that just because you CAN do something, just because you can have an effect, *even a positive one*, on something, doesn't mean you should act. Sometimes, even if everything else lines up and signs point to action as having a positive result, not acting may be best.

Given the sheer number of issues, problems, and conundrums in which we can find ourselves daily, it's sometimes in our best interests to not act. To use another cliché, "Pick your battles." Yes, you are a member of a community, a local and global society, but you can't take on everything, even if you have a stake in the claim.

Make sure you're focusing on YOUR issues. Use The 15 Minute Master as it's intended: to provide clarity and an action plan for you to make things better for *your* life. Although we've addressed a lot of times when you shouldn't act, the intent is the same—to offer you the time and a template to handle your own stuff, without becoming distracted by everyone else's everything.

Once you determine where you shouldn't be acting, the path toward managing your own issues and finding steps toward solutions becomes easier, and clearer. If you've spent your allotted time with the "What can I do?" question, you'll have a reasonable number of options for moving forward. When you've decided that action is appropriate, that the issue at hand is actually your business and acting is in your best interests, you'll be able to look at your options and appropriately ask the question, "What should I do?" with clarity and little time wasted.

Let's assume you've decided you should act. Here are a few guidelines for determining what you should do. It's easy to be swayed by options and variables. Keep it simple: What you should do is whatever moves you toward the desired outcome with the least possible amount of effort, wasted time, and pain (emotional, physical, or otherwise).

Remember, we're talking about ONE thing here. One step, one movement that makes things just a little bit better. It's certainly advisable to think about what might happen next when determining what you should do. Just know that those pesky variables—the "other stuff" previously discussed—will make it impossible to know what's coming next. Don't get bogged down with what might happen after you act. Think it through, make a responsible decision that causes no harm, and go with it.

The "causes no harm" phrase is an interesting one, and calls up another point to consider, "consider" being the operative word. You should never move on a course of action that causes harm to other people, BUT remember this is about you and what's right for your life. You cannot make your decisions based on others' shortcomings, lack of action, or motivation. Don't try to put yourself into anyone else's head; that's NONE OF YOUR BUSINESS. If acting on your own behalf moves you forward while someone else stays put, that's NOT YOUR PROBLEM, provided you did no harm to anyone through your actions.

One of the benefits of The 15 Minute Master is it enables us to see clearly what is in our own best interests. When you're on the clock, needing to decide quickly what you can and should do, you're forced to cut to the chase, leaving out the what-ifs that don't directly figure into your situation. While no man is an island, at the end of the day, you are responsible for yourself, your decisions, and your actions.

When I'm deciding what's next, I like to keep three words in mind: Kind, honest, and responsible. If I can look at any decision and consequent action, and it meets those criteria, I know I'm good. I'm doing no harm, I'm truthful about what I want, need, and am doing, and I'm also being responsible for my own needs, desires and obligations. Act with a true heart and clear conscience, and what you SHOULD do will become clear, with your responsibility to yourself and the world fulfilled.

When deciding what's next, keep these three words in mind: kind, honest, and responsible.

Chapter 9
Question #3:
What Am I GOING to Do?

The Final Three Minutes

Okay, it's put up or shut up time. You've itemized what you CAN do, you've determined what you SHOULD do, now it's time to DO IT. With all the information you've amassed, with your careful thought and planning, the question becomes: What are you GOING TO DO?

The greatest blessing of our human selves is a brain that functions beyond instinct. It is capable of rational thought, able to anticipate future events and act accordingly. It can process a constant influx of information that allows us to live active, productive lives. It is capable of change should circumstances require. What a wonderful, amazing gift! Yet conversely, one of the greatest *trials* of our human selves is a brain that functions beyond instinct, offering us option after option, possibility after possibility, until we're so confused, we don't know what to do.

Instinct is highly underrated. Look at animals. They do what they need to survive and live in comfort, as best as possible, depending upon their circumstances. They do it, well, instinctively, without hemming or hawing, dithering or miring themselves in indecision. If there's grass to the left, a cow will go left. If it's cold, a rabbit will seek shelter. If there's danger a squirrel will run or hide. An animal does what it needs to do to survive and thrive without extensive thought. There is no "maybe" in an animal brain. There's just do or don't do, and the outcome is always designed to meet the animal's needs.

Instinct is highly underrated. There is no "maybe" in an animal brain. There's just do or don't do, and the outcome is always designed to meet the animal's needs.

You'd think that would be the case with us humans, too—at least in so far as we'd act to benefit ourselves. Yet given our ability to factor in endless variables and possibilities, we don't always act in our own best interests, if we act at all. Sometimes, the sheer number of options becomes paralyzing, keeping us stuck. Despite our greater intelligence, we can stand unmoving while the cow moves on to greener pastures.

And that becomes the secret to question number three. Don't overthink it. In most cases, it's unlikely that a singular action, particularly if you've done your due diligence in answering the first two questions, will blow you out of the water. By this point, you should have arrived at some conclusion that will move you toward a result that's good for you in some way. That's not to say there may not be pain involved. But rarely is a situation completely unsalvageable should you screw up. Which you could.

The possibility of crapping up a situation is just that, a possibility. There's an inherent risk in any movement. But there's also risk in standing still, namely, the risk of watching the world pass you by as you remain in what you assume is your safe place.

Most of us act or don't act based on our relationship with fear. In fact, it's easy to let your emotions drive your decision-making even after you've worked The 15 Minute Master program and thoughtfully reached a reasonable plan for an action step. If you're afraid of the consequences, you're less likely to act.

Should you find yourself resisting action, go back. Review your answers to the first two questions. Think about why this issue landed on your head in the first place. What did you determine was within your power to do? Did you decide you should act? If it's at all your business (let's assume it is, or you wouldn't be asking the third question of yourself anyway), remind yourself again why doing something—the specific something you decided was best—is the right course of action.

Remember that at this point, you've decided your action step meets the criteria of kind, honest, and responsible. However, that doesn't mean it will be easy, or that you won't be afraid to implement it. When you recall that it's likely your action will cause a reaction in someone or something, it's hard not to be concerned that you might create additional conflict, either accidentally or on purpose. Sometimes, that's just the way it is.

If you're debating any action, we can assume your issue is not fun, easy, or cut and dried. That said, your best bet may be choosing the action that meets a few criteria. Let's break it down.

What you're GOING to do should be guided by the following:

- What causes a manageable amount of fear while...

- Accomplishing the greatest result toward your good and...

- Is the best balance of needs, wants, and responsibilities.

Notice that no one thing will drive your decision making. If life were that simple, we'd all be cows. Rather, with our complex brains, consciences, social mores and patterns, relationships, and responsibilities, we act based on a myriad of elements that, when put together, will give us the best outcome.

That means that what you're going to do may not be the least scary of options. But when put up against what will give you the greatest result and is a good balance of needs, wants and responsibilities, it's your best choice.

It may be time to take a big leap, a big scary leap, in order to get the most out of your action. Remember, we are talking about one thing, one singular action, but given that every action will likely cause a reaction, you may be lighting a fuse. It's never an easy call to walk headlong into fear, but if you've spent time with the first two questions, if you've focused with intention, you'll know whether it's right to pull out a match.

However, arson isn't your primary motivation. Tempting as it may be in some circumstances, blowing things up isn't the goal, unless those things are destructive in themselves. What you're going to do must always have a focus on good—good for you and anyone else involved.

Notice that I didn't say, "happy."

Oh, to be happy. It's what we all aspire to, for ourselves and our children. Happiness is the Holy Grail, and as such it's elusive. Not only is it elusive, sometimes it's just not in the cards at all. Happy is frequently an accidental by-product, and often not of the original decision or action. It may take time for happy to show up, if it does at all. Happy is an ideal in a not-so-ideal world. It can be at the periphery of your decisions to act, but don't try to make it the centerpiece.

Sometimes, you have to take happy off the table and do what's right, which may end up making folks downright miserable, let alone happy. So, focus on good, with all of its implications.

But keep in mind that good is an end-game, not always visible at the outset. It's also sometimes a judgement call, because what's good for us may not be ideal for someone else. Therefore, what you're going to do should DO NO HARM to yourself or others. That's not to say there won't be pain—another cliché to hate, "No pain, no gain"—but the pain should be temporary and ultimately lead to good for all concerned. What you're going to do must be a balance of what you need and want while being responsible to yourself, others and this complex social world in which we live.

Sigh. Are you exhausted, yet?

By the time we run through all the requirements for implementing our one simple action, it's tempting to do nothing, also an option. But it's really not that hard to decide what to do.

DON'T BE A JERK.

When my son finally decided to get clean and sober (and make no mistake, without his own decision to act, I could do nothing to change his life), he attended a lot of meetings. One of the principles that simplified his road to recovery was this: Do the next right thing.

The next right thing will always, always benefit you in some way, either physically, monetarily, professionally, spiritually, etc. Intrinsic to doing the next right thing is the added benefit that it will do no harm to another. Again, that's not to say our action won't possibly cause pain, but there must always be good at the end of the road—good intention, good planned outcome, good feelings.

It's really not that hard to decide what to do next: Don't be a JERK.

Know also that provided you're doing no harm, it's acceptable to put your own needs first. Sometimes, it's absolutely, completely necessary. Just because a possible action might benefit others, while another choice benefits only you, it doesn't mean you must always choose to benefit the masses. You can occasionally act like royalty here if indulging yourself is what's best. It's okay to decide that what you're going to do is what *you* need right now, even if doing something else could benefit more people. You aren't in charge of or responsible for everyone else, so if once in a while you decide to put your needs first (again, doing no harm), go for it. And enjoy it while you do, as long as you're not a jerk about it.

Using "Don't be a jerk" and "Do the next right thing" as guideposts brings us right back to "Don't overthink it." While you must consider fear, results, needs, wants, and responsibilities before acting, give yourself some credit. Let's assume you're a pretty decent human and much of this is intrinsic to your makeup. For the purposes of putting The 15 Minute Master in program form it's necessary to spell it out, but don't sell yourself short. This stuff is already in you, which brings us to trust.

Wherever you are in life right now, it's a given that you've made both good and bad decisions. (The '80s permed hair that had me looking like a giant poodle—bad.) But unless you're working toward heading up an international drug cartel, we can assume that you've tried to do what's right along your journey. Consequently, you'll follow your own lead as you get to the "What am I GOING to do?" part of The 15 Minute Master.

When we find ourselves in crisis, or in any uncharted waters, our brains go into overdrive in search of a solution. We want to fix it, solve it, get rid of it, so equilibrium can return and we can sink back into our comfort zones. Yet, if the situation is actually a crisis, one that is new to our experiences, our lack of stored knowledge about what to do may send us into a tailspin, not to mention a panic.

Close your eyes, take a deep breath, exhale (through your mouth—much more satisfying), and TRUST YOURSELF. You are not an idiot. Sure, you may have made some boneheaded calls before, but all that dumbness and those mistakes have provided you with a roadmap of sorts, even if these current circumstances are new and scary.

Close your eyes, take a deep breath, exhale, and TRUST YOURSELF. You are not an idiot.

Using the guidelines of The 15 Minute Master, you can work through the particulars of this situation, no matter how unexpected or shocking, and create an action step, one that will be guided by the underlying principles on which you run your life.

The 15 Minute Master isn't intended to remake you. You're pretty great just as you are. What it will do, if you work through the system, is corral your panic, clear out the confusion, and provide you with a simple plan to move forward, while honoring who you are and what you hold dear.

As you continue to work the program, through various events and circumstances, it will even provide clarity in your definition of yourself. You'll see, as you decide what to do, where your priorities lie, which will make future decisions easier and faster to make and implement. You'll know what's important—to you and your life plan—and act accordingly.

You'll also see where you need to re-examine your priorities. Often, what we think is important to us, isn't. Have you ever decided on a goal and looked back in frustration as time passed and you got no closer? Why is that? Sit with The 15 Minute Master, go through the steps, and come up with your action step. Think about how that step has aligned with what you've done so far. If what you've decided to do is a 180 from what you've done up until now, two things are possible:

1. Your goal isn't a priority, and you've been making excuses as to why it's not happening,

2. It finally is a priority, and you've decided to do something about it.

Either way, The 15 Minute Master provides an opportunity to clarify the jumble of shoulds, shouldn'ts, wants, and needs, to start down a path of action, utilizing your moral compass and already formed ideas and opinions, about what's important to you.

Trust in yourself, combined with a format for decision-making, will help you not only get through the next 15 minutes, but lead to becoming who you want to be.

You're smart, you're a decent human, and you're committed to being kind, honest, and responsible. Whatever you decide you're GOING to do will be okay, but in case you need a little more help deciding, read on.

Chapter 10
The Case for Courage

Courage. Read that aloud, but in the voice of the Cowardly Lion from *The Wizard of Oz*. Not only is that the absolute best way to say the word, but it takes some of the sting out of what it means to have to be brave.

I don't like being brave. Being brave means something in my world is scary, and I have to deal with it. Being brave means I have to put on my superhero cape when I'd rather be in yoga pants sitting on the couch watching Netflix. Being brave is not fun, at least until the scary part is over and I feel good about having been brave. But seeking out situations in which I have to be brave? Can't I just swing by McDonald's drive through and eat food that's bad for me? Knowingly raising my cholesterol is brave enough for me.

Yet, I am brave. I'm brave every single time that I get out of bed and greet a new day. And so are you. I've had to be especially brave at certain points, such as when my son was in active addiction and every moment of my life was driven by the madness that had taken over his body and brain. We're all brave, yet we don't often realize it until we walk through the fire, take a look back and think, "How the hell did I do that?"

> **I'm brave every single time that I
> get out of bed and greet a new day.
> And so are you.**

Often, we're brave because we have no other choice. There's one way out, and it's terrifying. In fact, it seems the definition of bravery could be, "doing something even though you're scared to death." Take our friend the Cowardly Lion, for example. Lion bumbles and stumbles his way through Oz and into the witch's castle, not because he's brave, but because to him, there's no other choice.

Except there is. Lion could have elected to sing sayonara to his companions at any time. Yet he didn't, for one reason: Dorothy. In his case, being terrified and going forward anyway was worth the risk because he cared about Dorothy. In the end, he realized that he had courage all along; it simply never surfaced until he needed to call upon it because there was more at stake than living in his own safe zone, however comfortable that may have been.

Maybe this will be your case for courage, too. Maybe what's at stake is bigger than just you and your yoga pants.

When someone else and their welfare or wellbeing enter our equations, it's easier for us to think about courage than it is when we're the primary or only beneficiary of action, particularly if the action called for will take us far from our comfort zone. Love is a powerful motivator, as any parent knows, and it has allowed many an individual to leap into action who would otherwise be content to watch from a perch at a safe distance.

Conversely, our comfort zones are powerful motivators, too, and there's sometimes a case to be made for staying there. But when there's a choice between having courage and stepping into discomfort for at least a while to make a significant gain, it's usually better to close our eyes and jump.

Rarely will the consequences be wildly monumental. More often, a temporary, but in retrospect usually fleeting discomfort or fear accompanies the thing that requires courage. Have you ever had the experience of doing something that scared the pants off you and then, after it was done, thought, *What the heck was I so worried about?* Often, the buildup to bravery—the worry and fear—end up being far worse than the event itself.

The reason for this is again our magical, wildly complex brains. It's frighteningly easy to get caught in the what-ifs of a situation—what if *this* happens, what if *that* happens, what if it *all* happens…AAAAAAHHHHHH. But our reality is rarely as terrible as our fear of it. Thus, the case for courage is a sound one.

When you get right down to it, the amount of time we actually need to be brave is fleeting in itself. By some estimates, all it takes is 20 seconds of courage to make magic happen.

According to writer and real-life zoo owner, Benjamin Mee (author of *We Bought a Zoo*), "Sometimes all you need is twenty seconds of insane courage. Just literally twenty seconds of just embarrassing bravery. And I promise you, something great will come of it."

Obviously, in Mee's case, the consequences were monumental. I mean, the guy bought a zoo. But the life-changing magic that can happen when we embrace courage, when we do something bravely crazy, can make the outcome, even one that's monumental and a little scary, exciting and even really, really cool.

Once we're in the middle of our crazy, courageous decision, on the roller coaster headed toward monumental change, we may find ourselves fraught with second-guesses, screaming, "Aaaaahhh!!! What was I thinking?!" as we careen toward the unknown. It may be tempting to put on the brakes, to go back to comfy, cozy, and possibly bored, because we all know bored, and it's not always terrible. When our heads are spinning, all we may want is a return to equilibrium.

You could get that equilibrium, although it won't be exactly the same version you had before, should you give up and return to the known. You can always undo just enough to settle in again. Rarely is anything final, except death and taxes.

But I'm betting you won't want to.

The exhilaration of trying something new, the rush that courage gives our psyches, is usually motivation enough to keep going. If you're at all curious, you also want to know where you'll end up. Monumental journeys are unpredictable, which is what usually requires the courage in the first place. If we knew exactly what was going to happen, there wouldn't be much cause for bravery, would there?

It's a scary world, which makes it tempting to fly under the radar to stay out of everyone's crosshairs. Yet, opting for courage, choosing to risk and be brave, even when, or especially when we're frightened ("I'm frightened, Auntie Em, I'm frightened!"), leads to growth that's simply not possible when we stay put.

Clearly, I don't mean stupid decisions or unnecessary risks. We're talking about doing something scary that has great potential for growth, change, or good—for ourselves or others. When you arrive at the third question in The 15 Minute Master, "What are you GOING to do?" note how your options make you feel. You may not like the answer at which you've arrived. Being brave is never the easy way out. But it's usually the choice that makes you break out into a sweat that will bring the most return, the biggest gamble that provides the greatest win. When it's time to act, you may want to channel your inner Cowardly Lion and go for it. Courage!

Chapter 11
When Nothing is Best

Now that you're all take on the world and brave and stuff, let's throw another caveat into the mix. Sometimes bravery is over-rated, too.

Sometimes, amid crisis, it's all just too much. Too much pain, too much fear, too many complications. Sometimes, all you want to do is crawl into your bed and pull the covers up over your head. And sometimes, that's okay, too.

When my son was in active heroin addiction, my home was a cross between a battleground and an insane asylum. As anyone who has dealt with or lived with a drug addict knows, every moment has the potential for crisis. You live in a heightened state of awareness and readiness, which is probably akin to the state of mind of a soldier in battle. Will he attack your back, your flank, or come at you head on? Given the ways in which an addict will lie, steal, cheat, and manipulate, you have to be ready for anything.

But dear God, it's exhausting. And impossible. There were times, and I shudder to think of them now, when I knew my son was actively using and I chose not to do anything at that moment. I was just too tired, too depleted to act. Given that acting would have undoubtedly led to yet another hours-long screaming match, complete with circuitous arguments meant to confuse and frustrate me, I simply had no other choice. I just couldn't address the problem directly in that moment, and I'd probably make the same decision again.

Clear-headed now and with eyes wide open, I know those decisions not to act were not brave, at least not in the traditional sense. But bravery can take many forms, one of which is self-preservation, especially when choosing yourself over another may have serious consequences.

So, there were times during our "just get through the next 15 minutes" mandate that I did nothing, because I didn't have the strength to do anything else. During those times, when my goal was simply survival, I let myself avoid the crisis. I'd simply do something for myself like head to a drive-through for a bad-for-me fast food meal (really, is there anything better than a hot, salty French fry to make you feel better?), binge-watch a favorite show, or just take a nap, since sleep was the only true respite from the pain and fear.

In those moments, my attention to self-care was the best decision, the best action toward the greater good, my responsibilities, and the ultimate goal of helping my son and saving the rest of my family from being sucked into the whirlpool David had stirred into our world.

Was doing nothing brave? Maybe not, but it was necessary. Self-care is never the wrong choice when you're up against something big. Doing nothing about a problem in order to allow yourself to replenish your personal resources is essential to success, and occasionally, survival. Personally, those moments of respite served to fortify me for what was coming. And what was coming was ugly.

Sometime during David's descent into the madness of drugs, I came to an epiphany: No matter what I did, I would not be able to save my son. If throwing myself under a bus would have ended his addiction, I'd have done it. But it wouldn't. Neither would anything else I tried. I know, because I tried everything. Counseling, interventions, doctors, medications, reasoning, bargaining, pleading, threatening, crying. Nothing worked.

Not only did nothing work, but as David fell farther and farther away into the arms of heroin, I realized he was dragging me and my family with him.

Addicts' brains are scrambled, yet they are still master manipulators. It was only after I realized that I'd driven my son to a drug deal, after he pleaded that he just needed to "pay this guy some money he owed so the guy wouldn't come after" him and hurt him, that I knew just how deeply I was enmeshed in his world. And it had to stop.

I had driven my son to a drug deal. Looking back, I know I did it more than once, always after believing David's lies that he was in danger, and if he could only pay off this or that guy, he would be safe and could get his life back in order.

Yet, only when my son overdosed on pain medication (heroin wasn't available) and landed in the hospital with the potential of life-threatening liver damage did I find the opportunity to combine both action and inaction to help him and to save myself and my family.

The 15 Minute Master program grew out of the crisis I experienced with my son, yet I'll confess there was no sitting in my prepared, quiet place consciously and intentionally answering the three questions that informed my next move. I decided instinctively what action I had to take (remember the power of instinct?), and I did it. At that point, the 15-minute process itself had become instinctive. It was only later, after reflection, that I knew what I was doing was applicable beyond my own circumstances.

What I did next was simple, but not easy: I picked up the phone and arranged to get my son into treatment. The day he was released from the hospital, my husband and I told him his choice was to get in the car and go to rehab or find somewhere to stay, because he was not coming home. David argued, fought, yelled, and ultimately, got in the car.

We took him to rehab and then, I did nothing. I slept, I ate, I went out with my husband, I enjoyed time with my daughters, all because *I let the experts handle it*. When we're in a state of crisis, we feel as though we're alone, as if we must handle everything ourselves. In reality, there are people whose job it is to help you. Let them. Letting the experts handle it, while you indulge in necessary self-care is the most productive kind of "nothing" you can do.

By "doing nothing" and allowing myself time to heal, I built up reserves of strength. In removing myself from the front lines of the crisis, I cleared my mind, bringing renewed focus to my plan for what I would do next.

For their part, the experts—God love each and every one of them—became my team members, people who cost me nothing emotionally. I gave them facts, they gave me facts in return, and allowed me to shift some of my emotional burden to them.

When we're in a state of crisis, we feel as though we're alone, as if we must handle everything ourselves. In reality, there are people whose job it is to help you. Let them.

Doing "nothing" in a crisis also allows others to step up. You don't have to be, and can't be, the boss of everything. Acknowledge what's out of your control, your sphere of knowledge, or your influence and PASS THE BATON. When faced with the responsibility to be part of a solution, people usually rise to the occasion, naturally enticed by the opportunity to contribute in a meaningful way. If nothing else, choosing to do nothing and let others handle things sets a boundary, one that again allows you time to heal, get your head clear, or do whatever else you need before rejoining the fray.

During David's second stint in rehab (yes, it was a long, difficult road), I drew my line in the sand. At a joint counseling session, I told my son that while I loved him and would follow him to the edge, I would not follow him over, nor would I allow him to take his father or his sisters with him. He could live whatever life he chose, but if he chose a life of drugs, he would not live with us in his world. In so many words, I told David there would be a point at which I would do nothing if he chose drugs. Not because I didn't care, but because the greater good—that of my girls and their father—along with my own survival, depended on removing myself, and them, from his self-destruction.

I would never presume to say those words were a turning point for David, but they were for me. During the most challenging period of my life, I learned that sometimes, you must walk away. Sometimes, doing nothing is the only choice.

If, during your time with The 15 Minute Master, you determine that no matter what you actively do, you won't change the situation, and might even prolong it, perhaps doing nothing is the best choice for you to make things better. Perhaps you simply can't fix something for someone else. You can't solve the problem and maintaining the status quo by keeping up with everything you've done so far would only prolong the agony. It may be time to say, "I'm done." Then sit back and see what the other players bring to the game. Because there are almost always other players. Perhaps it's time to let one of them get up to bat to see what they can do.

If you get to the end of your 15 minutes, and your conclusion is, *I'm not doing a damn thing*, then sit back, have a glass of wine or beverage of choice, and take a rest. I'll bet you deserve one.

Chapter 12
Taking a Step Back

Fall back! Fall back! Retreat already!

Did you ever just want to get the heck out of a situation? You've created a plan, started a project, initiated a course of action, and now all you want to do is walk away?

Sometimes, that's exactly what you should do.

The idea of retreat comes saddled with negative connotations. Somehow, it's a bad thing, closely aligned with the rhyming word, defeat. Yet a retreat doesn't always signify a loss. Choosing to withdraw is not necessarily surrender, although that's not always a bad option either. Rather, choosing to back off can let others know that you've had enough, and by god, you're not going to take it anymore!

Retreat, as with courage and doing nothing, is simply an option. Once we remove the emotional weight of the word, it becomes another choice, one with benefits and downsides, like any other.

Retreat, as with courage and doing nothing, is simply an option. Once we remove the emotional weight of the word, it becomes another choice, one with benefits and downsides, like any other.

At the "What are you going to do?" stage of The 15 Minute Master, courage would appear to be the most obvious strategy for a win. It's aggressive, it implies strength and fortitude—all cool stuff. Courage would seem to be the "best" option to get what you want. Yet, as we've seen, sometimes doing nothing provides the best outcome, especially when you get to pair it with a nice chardonnay, while you watch someone else step up for a change.

Likewise, on occasion, the best thing you can do is get out, before things get worse and come crashing down around your ears. It might be time to retreat. Sometimes, that equates to defeat, or at least the possibility of one. Should defeat appear likely, it's sensible to step back, salvaging what you can while giving yourself a chance to regroup and figure out what you're going to do next.

Bear in mind that defeat isn't always permanent, nor is it always monumental. In fact, a defeat may be a blessing, especially if you encounter a brick wall that forces you to turn in a new direction you may not have considered, but which could bring with it new opportunities and blessings. Loss doesn't always follow a defeat. If it does, it may be less of a loss and more of a clearing of the path for your way forward. Holding onto things, literally or figuratively, so tightly that our hands and hearts are clenched closed, can keep us from receiving new blessings or opportunities.

Back in the days when my life was a series of different piles of caca, it was easy to feel like every obstacle meant defeat and loss. Temporarily, I suppose it did. Yet, often I was simply marching down a path that would be of no long-term benefit, for lack of knowledge, lack of experience, lack of focus. Looking back, I now see the temporary defeats helped me build a firmer foundation. I realized—Okay, this is what I'm *not* supposed to do, so let's take a step back and figure out what to try next. I could then eliminate what wasn't working to get closer to what would.

Loss isn't always negative. Anyone who has lost weight will confirm that loss can feel really, really good. Loss can make you lighter—physically, mentally, and emotionally—all of which clears the way for you to get into fighting shape to manage what's barreling toward you. I once read that a single pound of extra weight on the body equates to ten extra pounds of weight on your knees. (Now that I'm getting older, I'm fanatical about taking care of my knees.) Transferring that logic to mental weight, consider the space you can clear inside of your head for clarity and focus once you "lose" stuff that doesn't serve you. Shedding bad ideas, just like shedding pounds, makes your brain a lean, mean fighting machine. You're not defeated, you're ditching what didn't work so you can figure out what will.

Shedding bad ideas, just like shedding pounds, makes your brain a lean, mean fighting machine.

Yet, defeat isn't the only time retreat makes sense. One of my favorite definitions from Dictionary.com, parked amid military notions of the word and other negative interpretations, is this: "withdraw to a quiet or secluded place."

When I envision a retreat, I picture a waterfall cascading down a stone wall in some Zen-like setting. Wind chimes supply soft background music, birds chirp, and everyone walks barefoot, making not a sound as positive energy restores my soul and a George Clooney look-alike pool boy brings me a drink with a little umbrella in it.

Okay, clearly, I'm mixing a meditative sanctuary with a spa vacation and my celebrity crush, but you get the idea. A retreat, regardless of the specifics, is restorative in nature. You go on a retreat to replenish, regroup, restore—all of those "re" words that mean to do something again—in this case, get your mojo back.

As I'm big on words, I "thesaurus-ed" retreat and discovered some nouns that bolster the idea of a retreat as refuge, namely, a haven, hideaway, hideout, safe house, sanctuary, or shelter. Not a battleground to be found. Just reading that list makes me want to retreat from something. I mean, who doesn't want to hide out from life every once in a while?

During the summer, I'm blessed to spend lots of time at the beach. Way back when I was expecting our third child, my husband and I bought a vacation home at the Jersey shore, when we had no business buying anything more than diapers and formula. To this day, I can't imagine what the heck we were thinking (yes, we went with courage on that decision). But we took a leap, and that little house has been my haven, hideaway, shelter, safe house, and sanctuary for many, many years. Little recharges my battery like spending a few days at that house, walking on the beach, watching a sunset, and getting a dose of the perspective that standing in front of an ocean gives me—namely, the world is a whole lot bigger than me and my problems, and this, too, shall pass.

My retreats to the beach remind me to breathe, something I frequently forget to do when I'm amid a crisis. I'm not kidding. I literally catch myself holding my breath. During one particularly awful stretch, I would wake up in the middle of the night, gasping. It scared the hell out of me when I realized that I'd been holding my breath in my sleep, a residual effect of holding it during the day as I waited for the next blow to land.

Years ago, I began the practice of yoga (I needed to justify living in yoga pants). As anyone who practices yoga knows, breathing is a big deal. It's always about the breath, finding the rhythm of breath and body, mind and soul. As a former unbeliever, I can attest that slowing down to regularly take some deep, cleansing breaths is downright restorative. It clears my mind and enables me to refocus and recharge, in mini-bursts, throughout the day.

If taking breaks to breathe is helpful, imagine the benefits of stepping back for hours or days. Of course, the spa or resort retreat is rarely a feasible option in the midst of crisis or problems, but building mini-retreats into your life, week, or day is not only doable, but will give you the extra oomph to get back in the game refreshed and recharged. In fact, The 15 Minute Master was built on the concept of the 15-minute retreat. Living in crisis, with 15-minute increments being all we could manage, my husband and I became experts at 15-minute retreats; that was often all the time we had to refresh.

Whether a retreat means taking a walk, shutting off all electronic communication and diving into a good book, or getting into the car, driving to the shore or a local hotel, and hiding out for a day or so, do it. Do it without guilt, knowing that sometimes, walking away is not only the best, but the only way to move forward.

You're also allowed to walk away simply because you feel like it; there needn't be another goal.

Believe it or not, I am a professionally trained singer. I took voice lessons for many years from some amazing teachers who schooled me in vocal techniques and performance, while I studied opera, classical music, and of course, show tunes.

For decades, I sang on stages, in plays, and at church, becoming a staple at family and friends' weddings. I kid you not, I even played Sandy in the musical *Grease*, leather pants and all. (Now there's a picture you'll have to scrub from your brain.)

I had a voice reminiscent of Julie Andrews, but who are we kidding? There was, and always will be, only one Julie Andrews, and I'm not her. I knew early on what my limits were, and that I would never become famous for my singing, at least not outside of my own pond.

Still, performing was great, and I'd be lying if I said I didn't enjoy the attention. But it was also a heck of a lot of work, and eventually, I just got tired of it, especially when I found myself being asked to do more funerals than weddings. Ugh.

So, I walked away. It was a good run. I had a fabulous time, and I daresay I brought some people happiness with my voice, which I acknowledge was a gift from God. But it was exhausting. I was also experiencing some difficulty with my throat and was no longer happy with my sound. After decades of singing, or rather, practicing, obsessing, worrying, and then singing, I was ready to call it quits. (Even Julie Andrews knew when it was time to hang up her pipes.)

Oh, the wailing and gnashing of teeth—not from me, I was cool with my decision—the protests that flooded in from everyone else! No one could believe I'd willingly give up something that I was so good at (yeah, I was pretty good). When horrified astonishment didn't work, ("Oh my god, you're not singing?!") folks would hit me with guilt. After all, my voice was a gift from God. How could a good Catholic girl turn up her nose at a present from the Almighty?

Here's the thing: I appreciated my talent. I used it for good. I used it until I was, frankly, sick of using it, and then I decided to stop. Whatever punishment God saw fit to slap on me, I was willing to accept, because I was just tired. And you know what? God didn't smite me. No back-handed smack from the Almighty Smiter. Instead, I found other stuff to do, and more time to do it. Stuff I enjoyed. Stuff that challenged me, including writing this book, for one.

Making the decision to close one door didn't leave me in the dark; it lit a ton of candles.

Making the decision to close one door didn't leave me in the dark; it lit a ton of candles.

The decision to walk away from something—even if it's something at which you excel or loved at one point—is yours. I'll say it again: The decision is yours. No one aside from you knows how much time, energy, and angst you put into anything, and no one has the right to tell you how, when, or if it's time to hang it up, to walk away, to retreat.

Only you can make that decision. If it's the right one for you, heck, even if you're not sure it's the right one but you just need a break, then for heaven's sake, do it. Do it without letting anyone guilt, shame, or prod you into sticking with it. When it's time to get out, GET OUT. No looking back. (Sorry, personally invested in this one.)

Retreat is restorative, whether we intentionally choose it or not. See it as an option, a viable action step that will eventually move you forward. It's another tool in your toolbox toward building an intentional, focused life, 15 minutes at a time.

Chapter 13
Now What?

Here we are. You've worked The 15 Minute Master and come up with a single action step to make your situation better. You've implemented that action step and now....

Oh my god, NOW what do I do????

Now, you wait.

Remember when we talked about how other "stuff" always enters the equation? Well, this is where that happens. Any time you initiate any action, regardless of whether it's big, small, or in the middle, there will likely be a reaction. Something will happen in answer to what you've started. Until that answer arrives, there's not much else to do but wait. Except for this, of course:

DO NOT BE MARRIED TO OUTCOMES.

This is so crucial, I'm going to say it again:

DO NOT BE MARRIED TO OUTCOMES.

Any time we have a problem and we initiate a course of action in response to that problem, we're hoping for a certain outcome. It's nearly impossible not to, given that we can imagine how our situation could go, as well as how we really, really want it to go. The problem is that how we want it to go sometimes crashes head-long into how it could go, meaning our desired outcome was not at all what happened, leaving us anxious, frustrated, and maybe even a little pissed off. (I've been known to toss around a few rants when things didn't go my way.)

Outcomes, especially expected, desired outcomes, can be the poison dart in any plan. Sure, we all want things to go a certain way. We can see it, we can feel it, we want it, we deserve it, and so on. But that desired outcome doesn't always happen. When it doesn't, it can leave us bitter and unwilling to adjust, torpedoing our ship just as we're about to set sail.

Demanding a particular outcome and accepting nothing less puts us squarely back in the land of magical thinking. It's also a big, fat waste of time. Rarely does life deliver directly what we want. Think of your life like a road map. You're headed from point A to point B, but if you think you're gonna get there via a straight line, you're delusional. More likely, life will take you from A to M, back to F, all the way to W, and then maybe, maybe to B, but probably not.

Detaching from a desired outcome may be the best thing you can do to move your life forward, for one particular reason: Although our minds can imagine the future, as well as what we think is best for us, not only can't we predict what's ahead, we can't imagine all of the possible outcomes, and some of them could be so much better than what we were hoping for in the first place.

Detaching from a desired outcome may just be the best thing you can do to move your life forward. DO NOT BE MARRIED TO OUTCOMES!

By being married to a particular outcome or result, you might eliminate some really awesome possibilities that may surface if you could pry open your tiny mind to something happening that you didn't see coming.

Like a surprise.

When we were kids, we loved surprises because they were always good. Our parents were usually the purveyors of surprises, and since they loved us and wanted good things for us, the surprises were happy—gifts to us to brighten our world. Do you remember your little-kid reaction to the word, "Surprise!"? Your heart likely skipped a beat in joy.

But once we put on our grown-up pants, we found out that surprises aren't always pleasant, leading to our aversion to the unknown. We want to know what's coming and we want to control it. Now, if someone yells "Surprise!" at us, our hearts skip a beat in terror, and we duck and run for cover.

If we're honest, even when things go the way we expected or wanted, the ultimate result doesn't always measure up. It might, if we were in control of every aspect of the situation, but—see "other stuff"—we aren't. Consequently, we may get the result we thought we wanted, but in reality, it doesn't exactly fit our vision.

Did you ever see a dress or shoes online or in a store on a mannequin (remember those things called stores?) and you found yourself obsessed with having whatever it was, only to find that when you tried the thing on, it looked terrible on you? I once ordered a jumpsuit that looked spectacular on my niece, Ashley, only to find it looked awful on me. (That may have had something to do with the fact that Ashley is twenty-eight years younger than me, but still….)

I saw the outfit, I made an informed decision, I instituted the action of buying it, and for whatever reason, it just didn't work for me. So it may go with whatever outcome you firmly believe is the best answer to your current situation. Except that maybe it isn't.

Once you initiate your chosen action in response to The 15 Minute Master program, one of two things will happen: either the thing you wanted to happen, or some other thing. Regardless, your response should be the same—BE FLEXIBLE.

Once you initiate your chosen action in response to The 15 Minute Master program, one of two things will happen: the thing you wanted to happen, or some other thing. BE FLEXIBLE!

Obviously, you'll want to be flexible if your anticipated, desired, prayed for result doesn't manifest. Frankly, you don't have much choice. Nothing says stupid like not getting what you want, and instead of adjusting your course, you rant, rave, and try the same things to get to your desired end with likely the same result—i.e., the same or a slightly different version of *not* what you wanted.

In that case, you simply revisit The 15 Minute Master. Armed with your new information, come up with another action step, fully aware that the thing you wanted didn't work out FOR A REASON. That reason could be grounded in any number of things. It's worth revisiting the three questions to reconsider—now with new information in the form of whatever happened as a result of your initiated action step—why things went the way they did, and what your next move should be.

Is what you were seeking the right thing in the first place? Were your actions motivated by kindness, honesty, and responsibility? Should you have been sticking your nose in this particular business; was it really your problem? What can, should, and will you do next?

Moving forward may only take a tweak in your original plan, or an entirely new blueprint. Either way, you'll have to be flexible in your approach because, simply put, you didn't get what you wanted, so it's time to try something else.

But, let's say you did get what you wanted. Is it the right fit? After all, I ordered that jumpsuit; it was the size, color, and style I wanted, but when I got it—ugh. It was just wrong, and no amount of accessorizing, changing my shoes, or softening the lighting was going to make it right.

So, what do you do when you get what you thought you wanted and you find out that for whatever reason it's just wrong? Let's see…oh, yeah—BE FLEXIBLE.

Why isn't what you thought was the answer actually the right answer? The result of your action step is an answer, but before it arrives, it's really just a projection of what you think is going to make you happy, or solve your problem, or do whatever you had in mind as your original goal. Until the answer arrives, you're just speculating as to how it's going to make you feel, which is why when it finally arrives, it doesn't always feel right. Imagination is a powerful thing, but when we land there, we sometimes forget it's an alternate reality, and it's not a reality at all. As we plan our action step, we imagine what we think will be the best result, yet we don't really know. We can't know what the future will look like until it happens, which is exactly why sometimes the thing we wished for most in the world leaves us flat and disappointed.

Surprise.

Surprise, and boo. One of those nasty, grown-up surprises, the ones that disappoint so well, has just reared its ugly head. Not so fast to judge, please. I've become a firm believer that the cosmos has a way of disappointing us for a good reason; to turn us away from one thing and toward something else.

Sometimes, we become so enamored with our imaginary vision of the perfect thing that we can't even see the possibilities in the thing that may not be so perfect now, yet, with a little TLC, it's Charlie Brown's Christmas tree all over again, a shining beacon resulting from Snoopy winning a stupid contest that wasn't really the point in the first place. With a little flexibility and adjustment, suddenly everyone's singing *Hark the Herald Angels Sing*, and that sad little tree is the centerpiece of a lovely celebration.

We rarely, very rarely, get to the prize directly. When we're in crisis, even less so. We can imagine, plan, hope, expect, and dream, but reality, with its variables, demands a willingness to adjust, at any and every turn, and to move, even if it's in a direction we never knew we wanted to go.

Take me, for instance. Consider this book, the books that have come before, the speaking gigs, the TEDx talks, and pretty much everything I've accomplished in the past decade or so. None of it was part of a plan, at least not at first. At first, my focus was simply on survival. During the crisis involving David's addiction, the only thing that mattered was not standing still, as standing still risked being in line yet again for any lurking disaster.

We rarely get to the prize directly. When we're in crisis, even less so. We can imagine, plan, hope, expect, and dream, but reality, with its variables, demands a willingness to adjust, at any and every turn, and to move, even if it's in a direction we never knew we wanted to go.

But plan? HA! Careening from blow to blow didn't allow for a plan, not one with any longevity, or one that required much thought. There wasn't time for that. Thus, The 15 Minute Master was born. Having a goal of not being a stationary target, there was an incentive to try something, anything, that might change the scenario of misery, if only for a while.

So, when everything was falling apart, one of my (at the time, unconscious) 15 Minute Master planning sessions went sort of like this:

Oh my god, I simply cannot continue like this. What can I do to make something better? Obviously, I cannot cure my son. I cannot fix the tanking economy and save our family business. I cannot turn back the clock and avoid turning fifty, unless I step in front of a bus, which, admittedly has had some appeal, but nah. I cannot stop the internet from obliterating the small newspapers I've been writing for. So what? **I know! I'll start a blog!**

As far as the best laid plans go, that was not one of them. But it was a plan, of sorts. It was a plan to encourage some forward momentum, which I sorely needed, as staying still meant drowning in quicksand. It was a plan with movement, if not much direction, which was all I could manage. While it didn't address or solve any of my major issues, it gave me something to do—an action step. Although it didn't lead directly to solutions, it opened windows and doors that ultimately led to a shining new path headed somewhere toward my own Emerald City. (Another *Wizard of Oz* reference; I can't help myself.)

When we don't know where to go, or what to do, it's more important to do something, anything, rather than remain mired in muck. Once we commit to moving, to action, things happen as a result. Frequently these things lead to new opportunities, new ideas, new relationships, all of which give us the chance to begin to put our mess in our rearview mirror, if only temporarily. Even the temporary respite provided by doing something different can clear one's head of the incessant replaying of problems. Sometimes, that's all we need to come up with a new idea to address the main issue, as well as to re-energize us on all fronts.

Even the seemingly dumbest, most inane idea can lead to profound transformation, regardless of whether the plan you had when instituting it comes to fruition. When I decided to start the blog, *Not Ready for Granny Panties*, the plan was to create a blog and make a zillion dollars (because that's what I heard happened when people started blogs), thus solving my pressing problems with the tanking economy tearing up our business, the disappearance of my writing jobs, the feeling like a loser at fifty because I hadn't accomplished anything of merit (managed in therapy, thank you). I also believed that, God willing, the income would help us at least address my son's addiction as we'd have unlimited monetary resources to do so (which never works, as recovery is not about money, but I was desperate.)

Try to guess how much of that actually happened. None of it. Zero. At least not on the scale I'd planned and hoped. But what did happen was that in creating a place for my writing, I unwittingly launched a new career that over time, has led to multiple books, speaking engagements, and a platform where I can utilize my experiences to help others, which, honestly is what means the most to me.

Yet, the only way any of that other stuff happened was because I WASN'T MARRIED TO THE OUTCOME of my initial plan. I made a decision, initiated the plan, and then figuratively drove the car through the night, following the headlights as far as they would light the way, adjusting course as needed.

I love that analogy. I discovered it through my gal Anne Lamott again, quoting E.L. Doctorow, who noted that "Writing a novel is like driving a car at night. You can see only as far as your headlights, but you can make the whole trip that way." In her glorious book, *Bird by Bird*, Anne goes on to say, "This is right up there with the best advice on writing, or life, I have ever heard."

Think of it: you get in your car to drive at night. It's dark, so you can't see the entire road, but only as far as your headlights will illuminate. Yet, you keep going, trusting that the light you have will be enough to eventually get you where you want to go. There might be a detour here and there, but sooner or later, you'll arrive.

No matter how much of a grasp we think we have on a situation and its mitigating circumstances, we can never be absolutely certain of any outcome. Stubbornly adhering to what we want to happen almost always leads to disappointment, frustration, and further inertia. We fuss and fume about why we're still in the mess we're in, refusing to move out of our own way. Eventually, we realize that maybe we're being stopped in our tracks because there's something else ahead of us that our headlights haven't yet illuminated.

Blindly and hopefully (and yes, somewhat delusionally) taking that first step in starting a blog was SO not the answer to my problems. But it was something. That something, combined with being flexible, adjusting or changing course, and trying new things as opportunities came up, became my lurching, stumbling, not-always-pretty road to a life that's pretty cool, interesting, and fulfilling, one that I wouldn't trade now, but never, ever envisioned then.

Surprise! Yes, that little kid surprise manifested when I wasn't even looking, which is actually the coolest surprise of all.

While you're being flexible and not married to outcomes, here's another thing to consider: Check your disappointment at the door. (See "fuss and fume," above.) In fact, if possible, check the majority of your emotions at the door during your time with The 15 Minute Master. Few things derail effective planning—and subsequent progress or success—like excessive emotion.

Check the majority of your emotions at the door during your time with The 15 Minute Master. Few things derail effective planning—and subsequent progress or success—like excessive emotion.

Now, my ancestry is half Italian and half German. On a normal day, I can vacillate between tears, hysteria, and stubborn, pig-headed determination multiple times in an hour, so I know I'm asking a lot. But infusing our problems and challenges with emotion serves only to muddy the waters, influencing our action steps and choices, not always in a good way.

Clearly, we are emotional creatures. But when our emotions enter our decision-making process in a major way, we almost always get off-course. I've never quite been able to wrap my head around the idea that things are not good or bad, they just are. Some things, like major losses, or a child addicted to heroin, are quite obviously bad, to my mind. Yet, when deciding how to deal with the stuff life throws our way, stripping down emotional attachments and dealing with "just the facts, ma'am" provides a clear view to plan and react in ways that ultimately make things better. Granted, "better" is in itself a subjective word, but less pointed than good or bad.

Emotions influence thinking, plain and simple. When we're disappointed by an outcome, rather than objectively looking at why something went the way it did and adjusting accordingly, we may pout, rage, stubbornly refuse to alter course, letting our emotions take the lead, instead of assessing with a clear eye and mind. While I won't suggest that you stop feeling, I am charging you to put a pin in it when evaluating your next step. Being pissy rarely gets anyone anywhere, except stuck in more caca.

While I won't suggest that you stop feeling, I am charging you to put a pin in it when evaluating your next step. Being pissy rarely gets anyone anywhere, except stuck in more caca.

Okay. You've waited, divorced yourself from anticipated outcomes, and shelved your emotional attachment. Finally, something has happened in response to your initiated action step. What next?

Simple. It's time for another session with The 15 Minute Master.

If something has happened, you're essentially looking at a different situation, however slightly things have changed. How are you going to respond? What CAN you do? What SHOULD you do? What are you GOING to do?

Revisiting the three questions will once again allow you to evaluate where you are, where you want to go, and what you're going to do to make things—here's the essential word, again—better. Plus, you choose courage, nothing, or retreat based entirely on your new information and circumstances. Nothing is etched in stone. Unless a clear solution to your situation has presented itself as a result of your previous action step or other changing circumstances, you're not looking to save the world and resolve everything. Just make things better than they were, based on where you are at the current moment; that's all.

See? Simple. Not easy, not necessarily quick, except for the 15-minute part. Life often vacillates between moving too fast or too slow, rarely at the optimal pace, at least OUR optimal pace. Yet carving out time to assess where you are and where you can go with The 15 Minute Master gives you at least a slight grip on time, either slowing it down so you can think and breathe or moving things along by initiating some kind of action for change.

The act of repeating the process of The 15 Minute Master will eventually get you into a rhythm that will soon become natural. You'll retrain your mind to automatically begin addressing issues in a calmer, more efficient way that relieves you of excess emotional stress and makes things better, one action at a time. You'll find yourself stepping into the process without even thinking about it, internalizing, setting up boundaries, focusing, and moving forward with the intention of doing something, one thing, to make your situation better.

The interesting thing about internalizing The 15 Minute Master is the unintended, yet hugely favorable benefits. Less stress, less unnecessary emotional attachment, less mental noise, and more efficient, expedient problem-solving, or problem-bettering, to be more exact. As with any repeated action, the process will become a habit, one that lets you cut to the core of the issue, determine an action, and then release it until something changes the equation. You get precious time to focus on other things, be they important, or just fun, instead of spinning on your personal hamster wheel and driving yourself insane with angst-filled reruns and what-ifs.

Repetition of healthy habits can bring on a Zen state. So it is with repeating the system of The 15 Minute Master. With enough practice, immediately upon getting into your 15 Minute Master time frame, you'll exhale, no longer holding your breath. Your shoulders will come down from around your ears and you'll relax into your state of focus, which sounds contradictory, but isn't. You'll get into "the zone," that holy grail of states cherished by athletes, musicians, scientists—anyone who recognizes that boundaries, focus, and intention are an integral part of the process of achieving. You'll slide into your sweet spot, working The 15 Minute Master before you're even conscious of doing so, until it becomes part of you and part of your essential problem-solving process.

So, your "Now What?" is rather simple: lather, rinse, repeat. (I always wondered who was so dopey as to need instructions on how to wash their own hair, but I suppose it's a good rule to never assume anything.) Work the system. That's it. Pinpoint your issue, find your quiet place, ask the three questions, determine an action step, implement your action step, see what happens, and repeat. Work the system with as little excess emotion as possible, letting go of outcomes and being willing to accept and work with the evolution of your situation. Repeat until you've gotten where you want to go, or until the situation changes, or until you change your goal. Lather, rinse, repeat. To review, here's the entire 15 Minute Master system at a glance:

The 15 Minute Master

System Outline

Clear Your Physical & Mental Space

Create the Framework ~ The First 2 Minutes

Is it real?

Boundaries

Focus

Intention

What CAN I do? ~ The Next 5 Minutes

What SHOULD I do? ~ The Next 5 Minutes

What am I GOING to do? ~ The Last 3 Minutes

Implement Your Action Step

See what happens

(Do Not be Married to Outcomes!)

Work the system again until the issue is resolved.

Repeat as necessary.

Again, it's not rocket science. The 15 Minute Master is a simple system that worked consistently and within the parameters above will help you make things better, 15 minutes at a time. That's all there is to it.

Chapter 14
Shall We Try It?

Looks can be deceiving. Everyone knows that just because something looks a certain way, it doesn't mean that it is that way. (Ask the Trojans if something that looks like a horse is always just a horse.) Further, I'm a skeptic, even though I do believe in ghosts. Some things are not mutually exclusive. So, just to prove a point, how about we try a few sessions with The 15 Minute Master? We'll keep our examples general enough to test the process and prove the point that it works, listing possible answers to the three questions and deciding on a course of action based upon those responses. Once you see that I'm really not messing with you, feel free to insert your own specifics on the worksheet pages provided and make things better!

15 Minutes with Crisis

The Issue: My child is in crisis. I don't know what's happening, but I know it's not good. How can I make this better?

Remember that you aren't fixing this problem, for several reasons, not the least of which is that you don't yet know what's going on. So, what does "better" mean here? In this case, start at the beginning: Better may simply mean figuring out what you're up against. Keep the words, "kind, honest, and responsible" in your head. Set your two-minute timer, clear your physical and mental space, and let's build the framework.

Is this a real problem?

If you suspect something is amiss with your child other than teenage angst (and be aware, even seemingly normal teenage angst can be a sign of a deeper issue), and you have the evidence to back it up—falling grades, less interaction with friends, new "friends" you don't know, changes in demeanor or habits—then it's safe to say this is either a real problem or one worth investigating. Any time a loved one is possibly in danger, that's reason enough to look further.

So, yes, this is a real problem, the scope of which has yet to be determined. Now, set a boundary around the specific problem; focus without the coulda, woulda, shouldas; set a positive intention; set your timer for five minutes; and ask the first question.

What CAN I do?

Recall the essentials when asking this question:

- What is within my power?
- What skills do I have to address this?
- What resources can I bring to this?
- What is my level of control?

The challenge here is that you don't know exactly what you're up against. Therefore, your skill set, in terms of how effective you can be at eventually solving the problem, isn't really relevant yet. However, you do have the power to seek information, so that's where you start. How can you find out what's going on? Let's answer the questions above.

>**What is within my power?** Obviously, your power is limited, if you're talking about influencing the actions of any human being, especially your child, whose job it is to ignore you once they pass the age of eight. In this instance, your power, especially this early on, is generally limited to sleuthing and gathering information.

>**What skills do I have to address this?** That depends on how sneaky you are, how determined you are, and how brave you are, because what you're likely to discover has the potential to be ugly. Yet, don't short-change yourself. You have a skill set here; use it.

>**What resources can I bring to this?** Who do you know who may have common experience? Do you have a relationship with your child's friends or teachers? Can you do some online reading to gather information before you act?

>**What is my level of control?** Again, this is about fact-finding, so your level of controlling the entire situation is limited. However, your level of control in discovering what's going on is greater and this is where your power lies.

Once you answer the above questions, you then brainstorm ideas regarding what you CAN do. Write down whatever comes to mind; you'll filter things out later. Any possibility should be recorded and considered here.

Possible answers:

- I can ask my child directly what is going on.
- I can reach out to a trusted friend of my child's and tell them I am concerned, asking if there is something I should know.
- I can search my child's room for signs of a problem.
- I can search my child's social media for clues as to what is happening.
- I can reach out to my child's teachers or guidance counselors to ask for information.

Depending on what you've done so far, you can eliminate options depending on their effectiveness (have you talked to your child before and it got you exactly nowhere?), your comfort level (not quite cool with the invasion of privacy option?), or your willingness to bring others into the equation.

While dealing with David's heroin addiction, countless conversations had no effect. However, I was not above searching his room and scouring social media for any hint as to what was happening. I knew the stakes were high, even when I didn't know exactly what was going on. If sleuthing would help, I did it. I also was willing to reach out to his friends, and what I learned wasn't good.

You'll have to determine—based on your instincts and what you've already done and already know—what your best option is to get to better. But don't rule anything out completely just yet. Set the timer for an additional five minutes and move on to question two.

What SHOULD I do?

Remember, the basis for determining when and why we "SHOULD" act:

- Is this my problem?
- How does this affect me?
- Is this any of my business?
- Will acting make things better?
- Will not acting make things better?

The simple answer here is no, it isn't your problem, at least in so far as you aren't the one who is doing whatever it is your kid is doing. But, when your child is in crisis, no parent will deny that it is YOUR BUSINESS. It affects your child, as well as others whom you love. Therefore, you SHOULD act, as playing ostrich and sticking your head in the sand will not help, and will likely prolong the agony, if not allow things to get much, much worse. So, your answers to those questions would look something like this:

- Is this my problem? *Not directly, but it involves the health of my child, so yes.*

- How does this affect me? *I'm worried about my child and fear he is in danger.*

- Is this any of my business? *It is my child's well-being, so yes.*

- Will acting make things better? *I don't know, but I need to try.*

- Will not acting make things better? *Doing nothing will almost certainly make things worse.*

Remember that the simple answer to the question, "What SHOULD I do?" is either something or nothing. Given the answers above, you've determined that you have a problem that needs to be addressed. You've enumerated several options for what you CAN do about it, as well as decided that you SHOULD act on this. Does it sound elementary to write this out? Maybe. But during crises, we often need to remind ourselves that we should trust our instincts, and that we have a right to step in. Privacy has a place as children enter adolescence, but if we're talking your kid's life, embrace your right to do what you need to do.

In evaluating what you should do, notice that you lean in a direction almost instinctively. Sitting on your hands or retreating (remember our choices for action—courage, nothing, retreat), will only make things worse. Plus, there's a good chance you've traveled that road already—denial is the primary companion of parents with kids in self-created crises, i.e. drug use. You know you must do something. Trust your gut. Even if you don't know exactly how to proceed, you do know that this situation calls for courage. This brings us to the final question. Set your timer for the final three minutes.

What am I GOING to do?

And here's where you choose. What is the one action step that you are going to take to begin to solve this problem? Not solve it right now. *Begin* to solve it, and in beginning, make it BETTER—our magic word.

Out of the list of possibilities, let's say you've eliminated talking to your child and snooping, at least for now. You're left with options that involve reaching out to others—friends or teachers. In this case, you might want to avoid friends who are likely to tip off your child that you're looking into things. You can instead reach out to teachers to see if they've noticed changes or have additional information as to what may be going on. Or, your kid may have a friend with whom you have a particularly good relationship and would be willing to share information without telling your child. In that case, go for it and reach out to that friend. Just do SOMETHING. (Clearly, I'm emotionally invested in this example; forgive me.) Let's say you decide to answer this third question as follows:

- I am GOING to contact my child's teacher to gather more information.

Ding. Time's up. And you've done it—15 minutes to an action step. Now what? Well, now you do it. Implement the action. Once you've done so and something happens (with luck, more information, in this case), you sit back down with The 15 Minute Master, armed with your new information, and repeat the process to figure out what action to take next.

For the sake of taking this a step further, let's say you've spoken to your child's teacher and it's as you feared; you aren't the only one who sees a change and is concerned. The teacher expresses worry that something serious is going on. What now?

Revisit The 15 Minute Master.

You've already answered the basic questions. Yes, it's a real problem, and you should act. Your first action step confirmed your suspicions, and although you still don't know exactly what's up, the teacher's response should lead to the next reworking of the program, starting again with:

What CAN I do?

Your options are all those items not chosen in the first round, with some new possibilities added, such as:

- I can tell my child all of my concerns and request explanations for recent behaviors.

- I can demand that my child take a drug test.

- I can demand that my child visit a counselor with me present.

In revisiting the question, "What SHOULD I do?" you may decide that a drug test is too extreme (although it probably isn't), but you know additional action is warranted. You may also know a conversation will get you nowhere. In that case, the answer to question #3, "What am I GOING to do?" might be a visit to a counselor specializing in adolescent issues. (As before, you can make the case for courage, nothing, or retreat, but in this case, courage is called for.)

Implement the step, detach as much as possible, don't be married to a particular outcome, and see what happens. Repeat when new information comes your way.

Obviously, this example is basic, the beginning of a challenging, highly emotional situation. We're simply trying to get some footing with this one. Were this real-life, there would be other mitigating factors and details regarding a child in crisis. This is where the particulars of your situation, your values, your needs, your resources—everything you bring to the table—combine to form your unique issue, as well as inform your answers about how to make things better. Still, know that regardless of the details, the system, in spite of or perhaps because of its simplicity, works.

And that, my friends, is that. As noted, while writing all of this out may seem elementary, you're formulating and executing a plan to eventually, and hopefully, solve a problem, if it's solvable. Consequently, approaching the situation logically, systematically, and unemotionally, writing things down as you proceed, establishes a framework. You can return to it, over and over, all while seeing where you were, how far you've come, and adjusting as you go.

Now for a few more examples, less stressful in nature, to give you an idea of how The 15 Minute Master works for more common problems, as well as crises.

15 Minutes with Work

The Issue: I like my job and what I do, but there's nowhere to advance in my company and I'm becoming frustrated.

Not a mind-bender, but a common concern. Depending on whether you want more money, or more and diverse responsibility, your focus will vary. You'll have to determine what's important to you, which The 15 Minute Master process will encourage. Here we go....

Set up your physical/mental space, and create the framework, which, after answering the question below, includes putting a boundary around the exact issue, focusing and releasing what might have been, and setting an intention for a positive outcome. Now, within your two allotted minutes, answer this:

Is this a real problem?

Well, you're thinking about it, so something's up. But is this the *actual* problem? This is where you determine if your frustration is solely about work, or something else. Is it about your position not being interesting or challenging enough, a lack of growth potential, or money? Or is something else at play in your life—something that indicative of a more general malaise with your circumstances both in and outside of work? Once you decide that yes, it's work and the lack of advancement opportunity is the main issue, you can set aside the next 5 minutes and ask question number one:

What CAN I do?

Again, the essentials:

- What is within my power?
- What skills do I have to address this?
- What resources can I bring to this?
- What is my level of control?

This example is a matter of figuring out what's possible in your work situation, what you really want, and what you'll accept as an outcome. At the outset, you're still on a fact-finding mission, so your level of control and power are limited until you gather more information to determine potential options for change within your workplace.

What is within my power? At this point, you have little power to change anything significantly, as you're figuring out where you stand and what you want. However, as in the example before, you do have the power to gather information.

What skills do I have to address this? Yes, you're still gathering information, but if you're good at your job and valued at work, count that as a skill here. Use that to present yourself in a positive light. Further, think about your communication style/skills. How can you use them to be clear and communicate your concerns? If you're strong at research, you could begin checking out options for change, too.

What resources can I bring to this? Again, your value to the company is a resource, as is your ability to say what you want. Can you arm yourself with information about your industry, opportunities in your area? Do you know others in your line of work?

What is my level of control? With fact-finding, the likelihood of significant change is small, and should be. You don't want to make an ill-informed decision. Your control is in your ability to discover as many facts as possible.

Now you're equipped to brainstorm about what you CAN do in this case.

Possible answers:

- I can stay put and enjoy my work life as-is.
- I can ask for more responsibility or new projects to increase my skill set.
- I can look for a new job.
- I can network and see what others with my skill set are doing.
- I can request a raise, using what I've learned about the industry to make my case.
- I can look for a part-time job for more money.
- I can join a group or find a hobby to increase my satisfaction outside of work.

In reviewing your list, you'll decide what's important—money, advancement, happiness, or some combination of the three. Once you see where your focus is, you can better determine your course of action. Now for the next five minutes and question two:

What SHOULD I do?

The point of clarifying what you SHOULD do is to further determine your investment in the given situation and whether or not you should act, be brave, do nothing, or retreat.

When and why *should* I act?

- **Is this my problem?** *Yes, this is your problem. Directly.*

- **How does this affect me?** *You're not happy about your work, which is affecting your attitude and behavior.*

- **Is this any of my business?** *Yes, it's your business. You're the lead character.*

- **Will acting make things better?** *Depends on what you want.*

- **Will not acting make things better?** *Depends on what you want.*

So, yes, this concerns you, it's your business, and not doing anything means maintaining the status quo, living in a state of inertia, and waiting until something happens to change the game and your circumstances. But if you want some say in how your life turns out, then DO SOMETHING. Simply put, you SHOULD act. Review the list of what you CAN do and pick something, preferably something involving action if you want a change in your situation.

As you go through your options, remember to read them aloud. The sound of words coming from our mouths can be almost tactile. You can feel them resonate. If they don't feel right, you're saying something that's not sitting well with you for some reason. Have you ever had the experience of being in the middle of a sentence and wishing fervently that you could reel the words back in? Don't ignore that. Look a little deeper and see what's really going on. If an option makes you wince before you've even done it, it's likely not the right choice at the moment. Think about the options of courage, nothing, or retreat. What feels right?

Now that you've thought it through, talked it out and come up with reasonable options for action, it's time for question three and the last three minutes:

What am I GOING to do?

Obviously, your response will depend on your answers to the above. If you've set boundaries, focused, and acted with intention, your action step will resonate with what's best for you at this particular time, which is all that matters. The future will come, and things can be adjusted down the road. But for what you know about what you want right now, what are you GOING to do?

Let's assume you've determined that it is all about work and that advancement is important, but you're not ready to jump ship just yet. This may be your answer to question three:

- I am GOING to speak to my boss and determine if I can take on additional responsibilities or learn about a different area of the company.

Now, you act, wait, see what happens, and repeat the process, figuring any new information into the equation, re-evaluating, and determining a new action step accordingly. That may mean a major adjustment, especially if your boss replies that yes, they think you're wonderful, but you aren't going anywhere, as there's nowhere to go. That information will change the game significantly.

You'll have to adjust your responses to reflect moving on, if that's what you decide, or staying put and finding another source of fulfillment, if leaving is more than you're ready for.

Take the information you receive, re-evaluate by working the program and come up with your next action step. Begin, see it through, and repeat.

15 Minutes with Relationships

Let's take a slightly different tack with this next example. The issue revolves not around you, necessarily, but your child.

The Issue: My daughter is in a relationship with a guy who is not right for her.

Okay, right off the bat, there's a problem here, and it's pretty obvious, but let's work the steps, just to see how this goes. Work your first two minutes.

Is this a real problem?

That depends on facts, which we have a tendency to misinterpret and misuse at our convenience where our children are concerned. So what are the facts? Is this guy abusive? Then certainly this is a real problem. But if he's lazy or unmotivated (your interpretation), has the personality of a wet mop (maybe just around you), is from a family that doesn't meet your standards (!), or just doesn't seem right for your child (again, your conclusion), then maybe it isn't a real problem. For the sake of argument, let's say that he's not abusive, but it's just making you crazy and you're about to step into it. So, set your boundaries, focus, intention, and move forward.

What CAN I do?

Here's the list of parameters:

- What is within my power?
- What skills do I have to address this?
- What resources can I bring to this?
- What is my level of control?

This is going to be dicey. Answers to the above might read like this:

What is within my power? Consider some mitigating factors. First, how old is your daughter? If she's fourteen, that leads to one set of options. If she's twenty-four, well, that's a whole different story. What kind of relationship do you have with your child? Does she listen to you? Only you can determine how much influence you have, and even then, it may not be what you think.

What skills do I have to address this? Do you communicate effectively? If not, now's the time to learn.

What resources can I bring to this? Read and research. Even though this is your child, there are ways of addressing sensitive issues that are more effective than others. Respectful communication, even with a fourteen-year-old, is key. Do you have friends who've experienced something similar? Ask their advice.

What is my level of control? This is a loaded question, so tread lightly. Truthfully, you have little real control, because even if you're dealing with a four-teen-year-old, she'll find a way to defy you if she wants to. A power-play is probably not the right approach.

Given the above, the list of possible answers to "What CAN I do?" is likely brief, as for now, you have one option brief, and that is:

- I can have a conversation with my child and express my concerns.

Demanding that she stop seeing the guy, or bringing others into this situation this early on is a recipe for disaster, but so might be you sticking your nose into this in the first place. Let's move onto the next five minutes and question #2, which is really the heart of this scenario.

What SHOULD I do?

You really, really want to do something here. I mean, this is your daughter, and she deserves better, and this guy is a loser, and on and on and on. Just because you WANT to do something, doesn't mean you SHOULD. Let's dig down and figure this out.

- **Is this my problem?** *Well, you're not dating the guy, so technically, no. But tell that to any mama bear and see if that stops her.*

- **How does this affect me?** *Since this is your child, of course it affects you, as it's keeping you up at night. But unless your child is about to make the mistake of a lifetime—in your opinion—maybe this doesn't affect you.*

- **Is this any of my business?** *Sigh. Yes, no, and everything in between, but only because you have your child's best interests at heart. And if that's the case, and you've raised a competent adult, maybe this isn't your business. Of course, if your daughter is fourteen and you're still teaching her things, then maybe it is.*

- **Will acting make things better?** *That depends almost entirely on how you act. If you're going to be demanding and insulting, then, no. But if you're sensitive and speaking entirely from a perspective of love and respect, then maybe.*

- **Will not acting make things better?** *If you've raised the issue before and gotten strong pushback, then acting again will likely exacerbate things. Be there for support, and leave it at that, unless you see significant reason to intervene. If you haven't broached the subject yet, it could be okay to dip your toe in these sensitive waters.*

Notice how the particulars of this situation change the focus of your evaluation. This issue is emotion-packed, and so deserves a different approach and emphasis than the one before involving work. This is precisely why working through The 15 Minute Master and writing everything down with a critical, precise eye provides clarity and direction. In the above situation, the determining factors of whether to embrace courage, do nothing, or retreat take on a different impact than before and should be handled accordingly.

Finally, it's on to the last three minutes and question #3:

What am I GOING to do?

I am *really* hesitant to even speculate here, as I've been in this situation and at different times things have gone well or very badly. But this isn't about me, so let's say that after all of the above, you choose:

- I am GOING to have a caring, respectful conversation with my daughter about my concerns.

First of all, good luck, and second, well done, at least as far as working through the method goes. Now, as before, implement your action step, wait for the results and re-evaluate as more information is provided. And again, GOOD LUCK.

Notice how, with different situations, different elements of The 15 Minute Master resonate. One of the great benefits of a somewhat scientific (fact-finding and recording) approach to challenges is the opportunity to determine exactly what you're dealing with, and then decide if action is warranted. As demonstrated, the work premise and relationship premise give rise to very different areas of emphasis. In the former, facts become the primary influence, while in the latter, it's your emotions. Thus, in the second case, whether you SHOULD act has different significance than in the first. Using The 15 Minute Master helps define mitigating circumstances and determine facts, clarifying options for action.

With the few examples above, you can see how working The 15 Minute Master method can help you clarify situations, remove emotion, and formulate one single action step to make things better. We've addressed Crisis, Work, and Relationships. The program works as well for issues like:

- Money

- Fear

- Doubt

- Goals

- Life Changes

And so on…

Let's lighten things up with one more example.

15 Minutes with Fun

The Issue: Work is hard, life is hard, and I'm not having any fun.

What a common lament. Though it may seem silly, fun is essential to a healthy mind, body, and life. Sometimes "silly" is exactly the point, although as grown-ups, we forget the benefits of fun.

As with all of these examples, your personal circumstances will dictate the particulars of your session with The 15 Minute Master. But for this example, let's say you're in a relationship, or even a long-term marriage, and life is kind of blah. Now what?

Set up your physical/mental space, your two-minute timer, then prepare to create a boundary around the issue, focus, make an intention for things to get better, and ask yourself:

Is this a real problem?

While it may seem trivial and almost childish to complain about not having any fun, pleasure, joy, and happiness are essential to a healthy, successful life. Yet, with never-ending responsibilities, shoulds, and shouldn'ts, fun takes a back seat or disappears altogether, making us miserable, exhausted, and frustrated. Yet, there are other reasons we feel those same things, so let's be sure it's a lack of fun and not something else that is the root problem. Once you determine that yep, I need to laugh more, get ready for the next five minutes and ask yourself this:

What CAN I do?

- What is within my power? *Lots, from joining a video gaming group to taking up parasailing or ballroom dancing.*

- What skills do I have to address this? *Depends on what you want to do, but everyone has the capacity to have fun.*

- What resources can I bring to this? *Fun can be free or have a cost, if you want to join a class, for example. What's your budget?*

- What is my level of control? *Again, lots. Although time or money may be in short supply, fun can be packed into minutes and cost nothing. Use your imagination!*

We can play with answers here, because it's within everyone's power to have fun. We all have some skill in the area even if we've forgotten how to use it. Fun can be free and doesn't have to drain your resources, and the level of control is up to you since you can find ways to bring fun to even the most mundane of circumstances. So....

Possible Answers:

- I can take a vacation.
- I can talk with my partner to see if s/he feels the same.
- I can find an activity for us to do together.
- I can take a class.
- I can start a monthly Friends' Night Out.
- I can do something physical (tennis, yoga, dance?) to feel better and get some exercise.

As with previous examples, look at your list and decide what you want or need to get the most out of your action step. Do you want or need to amp up the fun with your significant other? That would take some cooperation from your partner, so you'll need to see if s/he is on board. Or, would you rather have some alone time and learn something new? Make a list of possibilities and have some FUN with it!

As for question #2: What SHOULD I do? Here's the checklist of whether or not to act:

- Is this my problem? *Yep.*
- How does this affect me? *Well, I'm not having fun, which stinks.*
- Is this any of my business? *Yep.*
- Will acting make things better? *Yep.*
- Will not acting make things better? *No, because I still won't be having fun.*

This one's pretty simple. If you're not having fun and need some joy in your life, then yes, it's your problem, yes, it's affecting you, it's your business, and you really should do something. YES, act, already. Let's jump to the last three minutes and question #3:

What am I GOING to do?

In this example, the variables will be your time, the money/resources you're willing to expend, and any other person whose likes and dislikes you must take into account. Consider those, pick something, and have some fun, already! And if it doesn't work out, go back to your list and try something else. This is about fun, remember? Go for it!

Yet even with fun, proceed with thoughtfulness. Why thoughtfulness, even with something as innocuous as fun? Because nothing kills fun—or enthusiasm, or hope—faster than disappointment. Disappointment is the lurking shadow inherent in any plan or action, because things don't always work out as we want them to. So, just in case you forgot, here's the following, in bold, to remind you.

DO NOT BE MARRIED TO OUTCOMES

Every single time you work The 15 Minute Master, you'll clearly be invested in wanting something to happen. DO NOT BE MARRIED TO OUTCOMES. Of course, we all wish for a desired outcome, but as noted before, we can only imagine what effect an outcome will have; we can't really know. Something that sounds perfect may be exactly the wrong thing, even if it's what we wish for with all of our hearts.

So, work The 15 Minute Master, institute your action step and then wait, as unemotionally as possible, to see what happens next. Once it does, act accordingly. If it solves your problem, great! If not—more likely—revisit, reevaluate, rework the program, and try again.

You'll get there, you'll get there, you'll get there. Just not all at once and probably not the way you envisioned. Be patient with the process, with yourself, and watch life get better, 15 minutes at a time.

Chapter 15
The 15 Minute Master—Summing It Up

Fifteen Minutes. It's nothing, really, in the scope of time. But when it's all you have, all you can rely on to move yourself from horrific to meh, and then on to better, 15 minutes is everything. And it's all you really need.

I came to live as a 15 Minute Master backwards. Not because I chose to, but because I had *no* choice. That's how the system evolved for me. When living with the day-to-day horror of my son's addiction, I had no choice but to react in the moment.

The three questions came to me automatically, often in the form of *Oh my God, what can do?* Then *Should I do this, or will it make things worse?* And finally, *What am I going to do?* followed by a quickly implemented action step, all intended to simply survive the next fifteen minutes.

Awful as that was, I discovered the grace of living in the moment, not that it was peaceful—that came later. Yet living within a fifteen-minute time frame allowed me to regain some measure of control over a seemingly uncontrollable situation, even if the measure of that control was simply getting to minute sixteen. By focusing on fifteen minutes, I got through moments of intense crisis.

I discovered the grace of living in the moment. Living within a fifteen-minute time frame allowed me to regain some measure of control over a seemingly uncontrollable situation.

This organically grown habit saved me in crisis and works for me still, in crisis and otherwise. The 15 Minute Master is a valuable plan for tackling all sorts of stuff, even fun stuff, because yes, in this challenging world, we have to think about and often plan our fun. Setting aside time to figure out what's next is a balm in a world where so much is chaotic. It's fifteen minutes of sanity, in trouble or in play.

It's easy enough to live life in reactive mode, letting stuff happen and trying to manage everything on the fly, leaving you frazzled and frustrated. While it's impossible to plan out every detail of a day, focusing on a challenge and instituting a single step to move forward or start to resolve a problem can put the reins of control back in your hands, at least long enough for you to get your bearings, take a breath, and remember that this, too, shall pass.

Breathing is one of the gifts of The 15 Minute Master. Although every situation involves variables that can change the dynamic of what's happening, breaking down challenges into small, "reviewable" parts can help you see clearly enough to keep moving. Pretty soon, the big thing gets smaller or you figure out how to dance along with it. You breathe through your 15 minutes as you move ahead, getting back control, making things better a little at a time, and progressing to the end, whatever that may be.

It's precisely that uncertainty that makes The 15 Minute Master so user-friendly. You don't take on everything at once, you don't try to solve anything in its entirety. The awareness of change, other people, other "stuff," and how that might influence your outcomes means you get a break—from being in charge of everything, because, well, you aren't, and you can't be. So lighten up on yourself already.

The method makes your job simple. Not necessarily easy—remember, they're different. Just straightforward and simple. Two minutes determining if the problem is real, then setting a boundary, focus and an intention. The next five minutes on the question, "What CAN I do?" about it, followed by the next five minutes on "What SHOULD I do?" about it, ending with the last three minutes deciding, "What am I GOING to do?" about it. Implement your action step, wait and see what happens, and repeat as needed.

Brilliantly simple, and simply brilliant, if I do say so myself. Unflinchingly direct, unemotional, and concise, The 15 Minute Master takes you by the hand and provides a framework, road-map or system for getting through life's stuff—good, bad, and in-between.

As long as you detach from your desired outcomes and let life evolve, being willing to adjust course if necessary, the system works, despite whatever level of crazy you bring to the game (and

I've brought them all).

I've added several sample worksheets at the end of this book to encourage you to start using The 15 Minute Master to tackle your crises, issues, or daily life. By starting your relationship with the method right in this book, you can easily reference the how-to directions inside to guide your progress. Stick with the time frame, stick with the system, be kind to yourself, honest and responsible, and before you know it, The 15 Minute Master will become part of you and how you think, make decisions and act in this often confusing, overwhelming world.

Fifteen Minutes. It's nothing, really. Until it helps you make everything better 15 minutes at a time. Then, my friends, it's everything.

Fifteen Minutes. It's nothing, really. Until it helps you make everything better 15 minutes at a time. Then, my friends, it's everything.

Chapter 16
Worksheets

The 15 Minute Master

How to Make Everything Better 15 Minutes at a Time

The Issue: _____

_____

_____

The Framework (The first 2 minutes)

Is It Real? _____

_____

_____

The Boundary (Define the root):_____

_____

_____

State the Focus (Eliminate Coulda, Woulda, Shoulda):

_____

_____

What's My Intention? _____

_____

What CAN I do? (The next 5 minutes)

- What is within my power?
- What skills do I have to address this?
- What resources can I bring to this?
- What is my level of control?

_____

_____

_____

_____

_____

_____

_____

_____

_____

_____

_____

_____

What SHOULD I do? (The next 5 minutes)

- Is this my problem?
- How does this affect me?
- Is this any of my business?
- Will acting make things better?
- Will not acting make things better?

_____

_____

_____

_____

_____

_____

_____

_____

_____

_____

What am I GOING to do? (The last 3 minutes)

_____

_____

_____

_____

_____

_____

_____

_____

_____

_____

_____

Implement your action step. See what happens.
Work The 15 Minute Master again.

The 15 Minute Master

How to Make Everything Better 15 Minutes at a Time

The Issue: _____

_____

_____

The Framework (The first 2 minutes)

Is It Real? _____

_____

_____

The Boundary (Define the root):_____

_____

_____

State the Focus (Eliminate Coulda, Woulda, Shoulda):

_____

_____

What's My Intention? _____

_____

What CAN I do? (The next 5 minutes)

- What is within my power?
- What skills do I have to address this?
- What resources can I bring to this?
- What is my level of control?

_____

_____

_____

_____

_____

_____

_____

_____

_____

_____

_____

What SHOULD I do? (The next 5 minutes)

- Is this my problem?
- How does this affect me?
- Is this any of my business?
- Will acting make things better?
- Will not acting make things better?

_____

_____

_____

_____

_____

_____

_____

_____

_____

_____

What am I GOING to do? (The last 3 minutes)

_____

_____

_____

_____

_____

_____

_____

_____

_____

_____

_____

Implement your action step. See what happens.
Work The 15 Minute Master again.

The 15 Minute Master

How to Make Everything Better 15 Minutes at a Time

The Issue: _____

_____

_____

The Framework (The First 2 minutes)

Is It Real? _____

_____

_____

The Boundary (Define the root):_____

_____

_____

State the Focus (Eliminate Coulda, Woulda, Shoulda):

_____

_____

What's My Intention? _____

_____

What CAN I do? (The next 5 minutes)

- What is within my power?
- What skills do I have to address this?
- What resources can I bring to this?
- What is my level of control?

_____

_____

_____

_____

_____

_____

_____

_____

_____

_____

_____

What SHOULD I do? (The next 5 minutes)

- Is this my problem?
- How does this affect me?
- Is this any of my business?
- Will acting make things better?
- Will not acting make things better?

_____

_____

_____

_____

_____

_____

_____

_____

_____

_____

What am I GOING to do? (The last 3 minutes)

_____

_____

_____

_____

_____

_____

_____

_____

_____

_____

_____

Implement your action step. See what happens.
Work The 15 Minute Master again.

Acknowledgments

For me, life's main truth is this: There is nothing more important than family, friends, and love. Those who know me well will wonder what sappy creature commandeered my computer for these acknowledgments, but in my quiet, non-sarcastic moments (far between as they might be), it is the driving force behind everything I do.

So, I'll begin with my family. Husband Dave, who has loved me and put up with my particular brand of crazy for over four decades. Yes, honey, there is a special place in heaven for you. To my kids—David, Laura and Megan, who have brought me such joy and taught me everything important, thank you and I love you. To my daughter-in-law Kelly, and sons-in-law Jimmy and Mike, I couldn't have asked for better people to join our family. Thank you. To the babies: Emma, Luca, Jackson, Kaia, Nathan and the one newbie joining us soon, I am blessed beyond words to be your "Franny." There is no greater gift.

Thanks to my parents, Ann and Art Dettra. Mom, you've always been there for me and I thank you. Dad, you left us too soon and I miss you every day. To my siblings, their spouses and kids, you make my world brighter. Same for my cousins and extended family. How lucky are we to have each other?

For all those who have helped and encouraged me on this writing/speaking thing—my B.F.F. Chris Cherwien, Denise Whiteley, Jen Gardella, my 3 other chicks, Robyn Graham, Kristin Smedley, Kathy Marcino; my sister from another mother, Gina Rubel; Chrysa Smith, Laura Templeton, Jamie Broderick, Brenda Jankowski; and many others, I will always be grateful.

For those friends who offered reviews and encouragement, including those above, and especially Jen Croneberger, Fran Hauser, Dolores Hirschmann, Susan Rocco, Jennifer Robinson, Theresa Hummel-Krallinger, Beth Allen, Dr. Ellen Faulkner, Dr. Patricia Scott, and my high school singing partner and dear friend, Marie Herbert, I simply cannot thank you enough.

To my patient and wise editor, Laurel Garver, I really don't know what I'd do without you. You rein in my wandering, rambling style and make my work readable—thank God.

To Pat Achilles, my Granny Panties cohort, thank you for your artistic talent, vision and friendship.

To everyone reading this book, thank you, and I pray you find inspiration and help.

And finally, but most important, to my Higher Power, in Whom I find peace, hope and joy, thank you for this life and for the opportunity to be of service.

Love and thanks,

Mary Fran

www.maryfranbontempo.com

maryfran@maryfranbontempo.com

The Not Ready for Granny Panties lady!

www.achillesportfolio.com